Dictionary of Synonyms & Antonyms

Shabnam Gupta

Lotus Press
4735/22, Prakash Deep Building,
Ansari Road, Daryaganj,
New Delhi - 110002

Lotus Press : Publishers & Distributors
Unit No. 220, 2nd Floor, 4735/22, Prakash Deep Building,
Ansari Road, Darya Ganj, New Delhi- 110002
Ph.: 41325510, 098118-38000
• E-mail : lotuspress1984@gmail.com
www.lotuspress.co.in

Dictionary of Synonyms & Antonyms

ISBN: 978-81-8382-241-1

Printed & Published by : **Lotus Press Publishers & Distributors,** New Delhi-02

To

KARAN and SIDDHARTH

Your strength defies words

May God Always be with You!

FROM THE AUTHOR'S DESK

Having been a student of English Literature, I have always been fascinated with words and their usage. It is the unique interplay of words which can either strengthen or weaken our expression. While reading the books of famous novelists, what interested me the most was how they were able to weave a picture just with the help of words. These words are important tools, and I thought that a handbook which lists both synonyms and antonyms of a word in one place, without the needless turning of pages, would come in most handy. The compiling and editing of this has been as interesting as it was painstaking. I have my readers enjoy referring to this book as much as I enjoyed compiling it.

PREFACE

In the common words we use every day, souls of past races, the thoughts and feelings of individual men stand around us, not dead, but frozen into their attitudes like the courtiers in the garden of the Sleeping Beauty. —Owen Barfield, author (1898-1997)

Language is the bridge which we use to get across to another person. It is fascinating that language has so many roles — we play with it, argue about it, write about it, spar with it, and judge others on it. And you thought language was only for communicating?

Languages freely borrow words from one another. Often a borrowed word becomes so much a part of it that it becomes difficult to pinpoint its exact source. English, as we know it, borrows from at least a hundred different languages! Also, it takes on the local color and flavor of the country it is being spoken in.

Like every language, English also has its tools — words. These tools have to be used sensibly; else they become weapons. A sentence has its cast of characters, and each word has a role. What role is assigned to them and what functions they perform depend on the user's ability.

Turn the pages of this book and you'll never be at a loss for words.

— Author

CONTENTS

A

Abandon (verb)

syn – Relinquish, discontinue, waive, abdicate, leave, quit, evacuate, desert, discard.

eg.

- The unwed mother decided to *abandon* her child in the forest.
- Adam *relinquished* his post as the CEO after being involved in the controversy.
- The doctor decided to *discontinue* Bittu's treatment after three months.
- Mice *desert* the sinking ship.

ant – Pursue, chase, hunt, follow, undertake.

eg.

- Sri decided to *pursue* her further studies in the US.
- The big dog *chased* the cat out of the house.

Abase

syn – Degrade, demean, humble, humiliate, mor-tify.

eg.

- The girl felt *humiliated* by her sister's lack of attention.
- The officer tried to *demean* his junior by calling him names.

ant – Regard, commend, acclaim, extol, laud.

eg.

- I hold my uncle in great *regard*.
- The audience gave Surbhi a standing ovation after hearing the director's *commen-dation*.

Abate

syn – Decrease, lessen, moderate, diminish, subside, allay, slacken, subdue.

eg.

- The rain *diminished* the chances of India scoring a victory over Australia.
- The *decrease* in the population can be attributed to an increase in education and awareness.

ant – Increase, augment, magnify, enlarge, extend, dilate, expand, swell, grow, advance, develop, rise, ascent, heighten, intensify, aggravate, exag-gerate, spread.

eg.

- The tension in the walled city *increased* after the police shot down a Muslim boy.
- The company directors were worried to note that the employee turnover was on the *increase*.
- Suman's eyes *dilated* with fear.

Abbreviate

syn – Abridge, condense, shorten, truncate, trim, contract, shrink.

eg.

- The students were advised to *shorten* their answers and stick to the required word limit.
- The gardener *trimmed* the hedge to make it look symmetrical.

ant – Lengthen, extend, elongate, stretch, prolong, protract.

eg.

- Masood's tenure was *extended* for another five years.
- The interview *stret-ched* over two hours.
- The doctor hoped that the angioplasty would *prolong* the patient's life.

Abdicate

syn – Renounce, relinquish, resign, hand over, step down, give up.

eg.

- King Alfonso XIII *abdicated* in favor of his eldest son.

- The ailing dictator had to *give up* his throne for his successor.

ant – Accept.

eg.

- The boys *accepted* their responsibility in the whole episode.

Abduct

syn – Kidnap, carry off, snatch, steal, spirit away.

eg.

- The thief *snatched* the lady's purse and ran.
- The little girl was *spirited away* by her nanny before the stepmother arrived.

ant – Deliver, give away, surrender.

eg.

- The old man decided to *give away* his pro-perty to the orphan-age.
- The bandit *surrendered* to the police after his accomplice was caught.

Aberration

syn – Deviation, variation, distortion, anomaly, disorientation, error.

eg.

- Rahul narrated a *distorted* version of the whole episode.
- The manager pulled him up for his *errors.*

ant – Conformity.

eg.

- *Conformity* to the norms of society can stifle one's individu-ality.

Abet

syn – Aid, assist, support, encourage, incite, instigate.

eg.

- The generous *aid* provided by his uncle saw him through his rough days.
- Vibha was convicted by the court of aiding and *abetting* the murder of her friend.

ant – Hindrance, prevention, obstruction, interruption, interception, restriction, restraint, inhibition, prohibition, blockage, closure.

eg.

- Manju worked right through the day without *interruption.*
- The army has a transmitter device which is

used to *intercept* enemy radio signals.

Abhor

syn – Hate, dislike, loathe, despise, abominate, execrate, detest.

eg.

- Mahatma Gandhi preached that one should *hate* the sin and not the sinner.

- Huma's *dislike* for her stepfather was obvious to her friends.

ant – Love, fondness, attachment, liking inclination, desire, admiration, affection, passion, devotion, infatuation.

eg.

- All religions preach an unconditional *love* for our fellowmen.
- It was his *fondness* for dogs which led him to open a shelter for stray dogs.

Abide

syn – Stay, reside, continue, remain, settle, sojourn, attend, persist, tolerate, put up with, bear, stomach.

eg.

- The team had to *put up with* the tantrums of their star athlete.
- I agreed to *abide* by the rules of my company.

ant – Break, change.

eg.

- The class decided to *break* the long standing rule of their college and mass bunked.
- The new management agreed that it was time a few obsolete rules were *changed.*

Ability

syn – Power, competence, skill, efficiency, aptitude, talent, capacity, faculty.

eg.

- The artisans of Lucknow are famous for their *skill* in the 'chik-ankari' work.

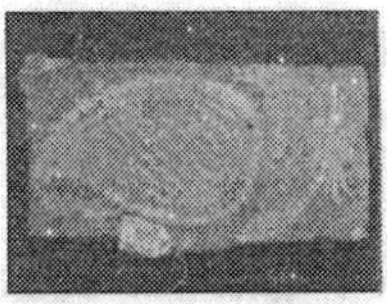

- The *competence* of a person can never be judged by his appearance.

ant – Inability.

eg.

- The director's *inability* to lead the company through the crisis led to its shutting down.

Abject

syn – Dismal, miserable, wretched, hopeless.

eg.

- The poor man felt quite *miserable* asking for alms.

- Shobha felt *wretched* when her brother teased her in front of her friends.

ant – Insolence, arrogance, haughtiness, pomposity, snobbery, domineering, defiance.

eg.

- His *insolence* with his superior cost him his job.
- Her *arrogance* made her lose all her friends.

Ablaze

Syn – On fire, alight, burning, blazing, in flames.

eg.

- The factory was up *in flames* by the time the fire brigade reached.
- Her yard was *ablaze* with summer flowers.

Able

syn – Talented, capable, competent, gifted, skilled.

eg.

- Shribha and Vasu are a *talented* couple and can play different musical instruments.

- The *capable* employee will get acknowle-dgement sooner or later.

ant – Disabled, incompetent, unskilled.

eg.

- Romesh was fired since he is *incompetent* and unwilling to learn.
- The *unskilled* laborer was not paid as well as the skilled ones.

Abnormal

syn – Aberrant, odd, eccentric, anomalous, unusual, insane, monstrous, irregular.

eg.

- Anubha's *eccentric* old uncle regaled her friends with stories right through the party.
- It was *unusual* for Dolly to miss her walking walk on the third consecutive day.

ant – Sane, reasonable, rational, normal, sound, lucid.

eg.

- Even insane men can be *lucid* at times.
- Though Akhilesh is a *reasonable* man, he refused to listen to his sister's pleas.

Abominable

syn – Repulsive, offensive, detestable, odious, low, vile, disgusting, obnoxious.

eg.

- I found the tramp sitting near the garbage dump *repulsive.*
- The guests found the behavior of their hostess most *offensive,* and decided never to come back again.

ant – Adorable, admirable, likeable, endearing.

eg.

- The little baby looked *adorable* as he smiled and gurgled at the visitors.

- Rishabh's *endearing* little sister has managed to charm all the teachers of her school.

Abound

syn – Bristle, crawl, flow, swarm, teem.

eg.

- Lokesh *bristled* with energy as he entered his new office.
- Locusts *swarmed* over the fields.

ant – Scarcity, absence.

eg.

- The *scarcity* of rains alarmed the farmers.
- *Absence* makes the heart grow fonder.

Abridgment

syn – Abbreviated, summary, digest, compendium, synopsis.

eg.

- The report *summary* explained the whole project quite well.
- Ayush did not have enough time, so he read the *synopsis* of the book before the exam.

ant – Elaborate, expand, elongate.

eg.

- The students requested the teacher to *elaborate* the theory of business cycles once again.
- Our shadows *elongate* in the afternoon sun.

Abscond

syn – Slip away, leave, decamp, depart, retreat, disappear, run away, flee, steal away, take oneself off, run off.

eg.

- Tara *slipped away* the moment the teacher turned her back.
- The thief *decamped* with the cash and jewelry.

ant – Hold one's ground, reappear, present oneself, emerge, arrive, remain, be present, come into view, put in a reappearance.

eg.

- The Indian team *held its ground* against the Australians who were in full form.

- The crowds cheered when the beloved leader *reappeared* after years of self-imposed exile.

Absolute

syn – Total, complete, utter, unconditional, unlimited, supreme, arbitrary, tyrannical, autocratic, dictatorial, overbearing, fixed.

eg.

- The matriarch has *total* control over her wards.
- The despot was the *supreme* head of the country and his word was law.

ant – Limited, docile, lenient, mild, meek, yielding.

eg.

- Vishesh knew that the offer was for a *limited* period.
- The new nanny of the Sharmas looked quite *docile.*

Absorb

syn – Soak up, take in, assimilate, incorporate, ingest, receive.

eg.

- The squirrels were sitting on the grass, *soaking up* the afternoon sun.

- The company directors are going to *incorporate* a new clause in the agreement.

ant – Disgorge, dissipate, disperse, eject, emit, exude.

eg.

- The factory *emitted* noxious and foul-smelling gas.
- Heavy rains *disgorged* the boulder from its place.

Abstain

syn – Refrain, desist, withdraw, withhold, go without, forbear.

eg.

- Let us *refrain* from speaking ill about others.
- Rakesh has pledged to *go without* alcohol for a month.

ant – Pursue, adopt, persist, offer.

eg.

- We must *persist* on the right path despite resistance.
- The government has *adopted* a new set of rules and regulations for small and medium business enterprises.

Absurd

syn – Foolish, silly, stupid, ridiculous, strange, irrational, incongruous, senseless, silly.

eg.

- I am not *stupid* enough to believe your tall stories.
- It is *ridiculous* for a business house to think of only profitability and not responsibility.

ant – Logical, sound, rational, sensible, consistent, reasonable.

eg.

- The Commander knew it was *sensible* to wait for daylight to commence attack on the enemy.
- Hari's proposition seemed quite *sound* to the board of directors.

Accept

syn – Believe, confirm, allow, assent, agree, honor, admit, take, acknowledge.

eg.

- Isha will *agree* to Mohan's proposal if her parents like him enough.
- Appu *admitted* his mistake to the headmaster.

ant – Disbelieve, reject, refuse, disagree, nonconsent, deny.

eg.

- There is no reason to *disbelieve* Kamini's story.
- Sukhi *refused* to take up my offer.

Accompany

syn – Escort, go along with, join, attend, chaperon, conduct, convoy, consort.

eg.

- The Boy Scouts decided to *go along with* the housemaster's decision for the mission.

- The actor was *escorted* by his bodyguard.

ant – Discard, leave, abandon, desert.

eg.

- Pooja plans to *discard* an old pair of shoes every time she buys a new one.
- One should *leave* bad habits if one wants to rise in life.

Accumulate

syn – Assemble, accrue, amass, collect, gather, congregate, hoard, store, rally, convene, add.

eg.

- The delegates *assembled* in the auditorium at the appointed hour.
- The squirrels *hoard* and save nuts for the winter.

ant – Disperse, scatter, broadcast, spread, dissipate, distribute.

eg.

- The wind blows and *disperses* the seeds.
- There was *scattered* rain right through the country.

Accurate

syn – Correct, precise, exact, perfect, nice, right, true.

eg.

- The teacher wanted the *correct* solution to the problem.

- The police confirmed the *precise* time at which the criminal had entered the building.

ant – Incorrect, inaccurate, erroneous, inexact, wrong, false.

eg.

- The lawyer provided *erroneous* information to save his client.
- The *incorrect* data led to the *wrong* conclusions.

Accuse

Syn – Arraign, impeach, charge, incriminate, indict.

eg.

- Shubh was *charged* with reckless driving by the police.
- Brad was *incriminated* by an eye witness who had seen him at the scene of crime.

Ant - Exonerate, pardon, clear, absolve.

eg.

- The judge *exonerated* Ayush of the crime.
- The state granted him *pardon.*

Achieve

syn – Attain, accomplish, do, reach, win, effect, fulfill, realize, gain, perform, finish, execute, acquire.

eg.

- An attentive person can *accomplish* as much in an hour as an inattentive one will not achieve even in a day.
- Maqsood always *executes* the orders promptly.

ant – Fail, miss, miscarry.

eg.

- The school has adopted a policy not to fail any student until class VII.
- Arti *missed* first division by a few marks.

Acknowledge

syn – Admit, own, grant, accept, profess, recognize, concede, confess, allow.

eg.

- Ankit *owned up* blame for the mistakes in his project.
- The company *recognizes* the rights of its employees.

ant – Contradict, foreswear, disown, deny, disclaim.

eg.

- The team *disowned* responsibility for the theft in the locker.

- The witness *contradicted* his own story in a moment of panic.

Acquaintance

syn – Friendship, associate, friend, contact, knowledge, familiarity.

eg.

- His *friendship* with the rival business house was his undoing.
- It is often said that *familiarity* breeds contempt.

ant – Enmity, ignor-ance, hostility, lack of knowledge.

eg.

- Anju's *enmity* with Sudha was the talk of the town.
- The scientist confessed his *ignorance* of the newest development in his field of research.

Acquistion

syn – Accumulation, appropriation, obtain, ownership, proprietorship, attainment; purchase, gain, profit, earning; recovery, redemption.

eg.

- Somesh *purchased* the land on his wife's name to avail tax benefits.
- Gambhir made a good *profit* by trading in shares.

ant – loss, consumption, decrease, exhaustion, depletion, expenditure, forfeiture, squandering, waste, deprivation, relinqui-shment, surrender, disbur-sement, outgoings, spend-ing.

eg.

- If we continue to *waste* our natural resources, our future generations will have neither enough water nor electricity.
- Purab advised his wife to curb her *expen-diture.*

Act

Syn – Action, deed, exploit, feat, operation, performance.

eg.

- Mother insists that we do one good *deed* every day.
- When he climbed the highest mountain peak, his *feat* was unmatched for years.

Actual

syn – Authentic, real, certain, definite, tangible, demonstrable.

eg.

- Shuchi loved the taste of the *authentic* butter chicken gravy when she visited India.
- Vibhu was *definite* that she'd seen Payal in the market the day before.

ant – Fabulous, virtual, impossible.

eg.

- Naman tried to do the *impossible* by climbing the tree with one hand.

- Children try to tell *fabulous* stories to get out of sticky situations.

Admire

syn – Applaud, extol, approve, praise, esteem, think highly of.

eg.

- My English teacher always gives *praise* where it is due.
- Tarini was proud to hear the seniors *extol* her husband.

ant – Despise, blame, condemn, disapprove, critical.

eg.

- You are following the wrong path, so do not *blame* me for your downfall.
- It is wrong to *despise* someone for the color of the skin they are born with.

Adapt

syn – Fit, regulate, conform, suit, find your feet, settle in.

eg.

- The company heads wanted clear rules to *regulate* the working and service conditions of the employees.

- The Sharmas have managed to *find their feet* in their new home in the UK in no time at all.

ant – Misfit, differ, disagree.

eg.

- Prabhu is a *misfit* for the work assigned to him.
- He *differs* from his colleagues in that his work is always up to the mark.

Adjust

syn – Set in order, arrange, set right, regulate, accommodate, settle, set, compose, fiddle, fine-tune, bend.

eg.

- It took him two hours to *arrange* the articles on his teacher's desk and set them right.
- Husbands and wives have to *accommodate* themselves to many unpleasant things in each other's nature if they want to be happy.

ant – Displace, dislocate, disjoint, derange, disconnect, disarrange.

eg.

- The robber ransacked the room and left everything *disarranged*.
- Constant transfers uproot the children and make them feel *displaced*.

Admit

syn – Own up, confess, divulge, avow, grant, concede, give, yield.

eg.

- The young boy *confessed* his feelings to the young girl he loved.
- The robber *owned up* his crime before the judge.

ant – Disown, deny, dispute, disavow, disclaim.

eg.

- The guards *denied* him entry to the conference since he did not have a valid invite.

- The couple *denied* that there were any *disputes* with the neighbors.

Adversity

syn – Affliction, hardship, misery, poverty, misfortune.

eg.

- *Hardship* is the test for endurance.
- *Poverty* is the root cause of all evil.

ant – Prosperity, luck, fortune, happiness.

eg.

- It gives me great *happiness* to announce the release of my new movie.
- Peace and *prosperity* marked the golden age of India.

Advice

syn – Warn, admonish, recommend, counsel, suggest, prompt.

eg.

- His teacher *admonished* him for not finishing his work on time.
- The judge *warned* Hari that his next theft would land him in jail for an indeterminate period.

ant – Deter, dissuade, restrain, hinder, discourage, criticize.

eg.

- The warning on the notice board served to *deter* the non-members from entering the club.
- I tried to *dissuade* my friend from settling down in the USA.

Afraid

syn – Frightened, alarmed, anxious, displeasure, scared, panicky, anxious, fearful, faint-hearted.

eg.

- The cat was *scared* after climbing the topmost branch of the tree.
- The little girl was *alarmed* when the car sped towards her.

ant – Brave, bold, courageous, unafraid, daring, upright.

eg.

- Atul is a *brave* boy and he wants to be a soldier when he grows up.

- The *courageous* girl gave a tough fight to the armed terrorists.

Affront

syn – Offend, insult, outrage, gall, provoke, displease.

eg.

- Pammy was *offended* when she was not invited for Ranjan's party.
- All the students of our class were punished when Surat *displeased* the teacher by asking too many questions.

ant – Praise, appease, pacify.

eg.

- The family members *praised* Qasim for handling the conflict situation so well.
- The crying baby was *pacified* when she got milk.

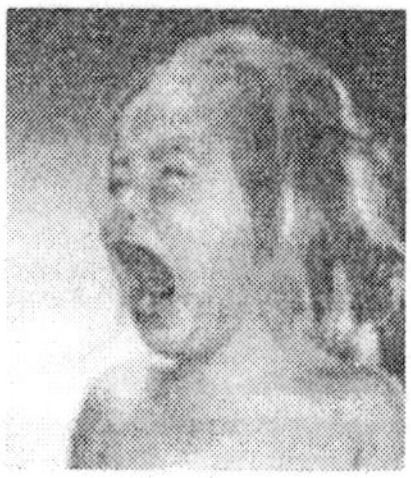

Alarming

syn – Frightful, terrible, ominous, disturbing, upsetting, shocking.

eg.

- The scene of the rail accident was *terrible.*
- The fight between the two good friends was *upsetting* for the whole class.

ant – Hopeful, bright, auspicious.

eg.

- The recent Indo-Pak decision on disarmament gives a *bright* picture of the future of a peaceful world.

- The bride and groom got married on an *auspicious* day.

Allay

syn – Repress, check, ease, lighten, subdue, calm, abate, soothe, relieve, palliate, dull, rid, soften, assuage.

eg.

- Anand *eased* the situation by admitting his fault.
- His soothing words could not *assuage* the feelings of the grieving widow.

ant – Aggravate, enhance, worsen, heighten.

eg.

- His timidity *aggravated* an already bad situation.
- The talks between the two leaders *worsened* the overall situation.

Allure

syn – Charm, tempt, seduce, beguile, solicit, win over, invite, entice, draw, fascinate, endear.

eg.

- Maneka's beauty *charmed* the stoic saint, Vishvamitra.

- The advertisements *seduce* the viewer by promising more than the products can deliver.

ant – Deter, repulse, rebuff, reject, disenchant, check.

eg.

- The noisy and rowdy children *repulsed* Vikram.
- It is a scientific fact that similar poles of a magnet *repel* each other.

Ally

syn – Friend, abettor, helper, supporter, spies, colleague, partner, accomplice, accessory, companion, cooperator.

eg.

- Sumitra and Ali have been close *friends* since their school days.
- The police caught one thief, but his *accomplice* managed to flee.

ant – Enemy, opponent, rival, competitor.

eg.

- The Indian army defends the country against *enemy* attack.
- The sumo wrestler had no chance against his formidable *opponent*.

Amazing

syn – Extraordinary, surprising, remarkable, miraculous, marvelous, wondrous, stupendous, wonderful, astounding.

eg.

- The patient made a *miraculous* recovery and surprised the doctors.
- The star-lit night sky looked *wonderful* to the young lovers.

ant – Ordinary, common, everyday, commonplace, average, habitual, usual.

eg.

- *Ordinary* citizens should be aware of their duties as well as responsibilities towards their country.
- Arvind is an *average* student but a brilliant sportsman.

Ambition

syn – Purpose, objective, aim, wish, hope, intention, ambition, goal, end, desire.

eg.

- It is his *ambition* to become the CEO of his company.
- The *purpose* of a good education is to empower you and prepare you for life.

ant – Indifference, purposelessness, aimlessness

eg.
- His *indifference* towards his family earned him the ire of everyone around.
- The *aimlessness* of the youth bothers the elders of the family.

Amalagamation

syn – Merger, mixture, join up, blending, mingle, union.

eg.
- The two companies signed up the *merger* agreement.
- Marriage is the holy *union* of two persons.

ant – Separation, partition, division, severance.

eg.
- The *separation* of the couple saddened the family members.
- The *partition* of India in 1947 was a sad day for Indians.

Ample

syn – Broad, full, unrestricted, plenty, sufficient, spacious, abundant, unlimited, extensive, large.

eg.
- The woman had a *broad* smile on her face.
- This year the crop has been *abundant*.

ant – Scarce, short, restricted, limited, insuff-icient, small, skimpy, narrow.

eg.
- When the supply of any product becomes *scarce* its price tends to rise.
- The coke was *limited*, so the children asked for juice.

Amuse

syn – Please, enliven, interest, absorb, engross, charm, cheer, entertain, keep amused, gladden.

eg.
- The charming speaker *enlivened* the workshop with his amusing anecdotes.

- Radhe was so *engrossed* in the book that he didn't see his brother enter the room.

ant – Bore, annoy, tire, fatigue, vex.

eg.

- The bureaucrat was such a *bore* that I couldn't hold back my yawn when I was with him.
- The child managed to *vex* his baby sitter in no time at all.

Ancestor

syn – Forbear, forefather, progenitor, antecedent, predecessor.

eg.

- Johnson's dictionary was the *progenitor* of dictionaries.
- The judge cited an *antecedent* for his judgment.

Ant - Descendants, offspring, progeny, brood.

eg.

- Welhams are *descendants* of William the Conqueror.
- Mother did not want to cart her brood to the supermarket, so she left us home.

Animal

syn – Beast, brute, creature, monster.

eg.

- Jack the Ripper was a *beast* with normorality.
- The police was admonished for using *brute* force on the witness.

Annexation

syn – Increase, expansion, supplement, augmentation, accession, extension, appendix.

eg.

- Science should *supplement* the efforts of the farmers to increase the quality and yield of the agricultural produce.
- The bank granted him an *extension* on the period of repayment of his loan

ant – Decrease, surrender, contraction, curtailment, subtraction, diminution, reduction, fall.

eg.

- The defeated kings decided to *surrender* to the victor.
- The engineer left a gap between rails to provide a margin for expansion and *contraction* of steel.

Annihilate

syn – Destroy, wipe out, suppress, extinguish, obliterate.

eg.

- The waste of natural resources will *wipe out* our planet sooner or later.
- The student *extinguished* the candle and the hall plunged in darkness.

ant – Establish, support, encourage, produce.

eg.

- The Geneva Conference of the super powers on disarmament *established* the need for an arms free world.
- India and other nonaligned countries have *supported* the move for a nuclear free outer space.

Annoy

syn – Worry, trouble, irritate, infuriate, disturb, aggravate, get on your nerves, harass, tease, bother, vex, torment.

eg.

- The opposition party *aggravated* the ruling party by raising slogans in front of the visiting dignitary.
- Her little brother *teased* her mercilessly.

ant – Please, charm, oblige, delight, gratify, gladden.

eg.

- She *pleased* the teacher with her sugar sweet comments.
- Her *charm* left the film director spellbound.

Answer

syn – Reply, retort, react, repartee, rejoinder, response, solution.

eg.

- Manchanda tries to *reply* to his business queries as soon as possible.
- His *retort* left the opponent speechless.

ant – Query, question, defiance, interrogation.

eg.

- The little boy's *questions* brought a smile to his mother's face.
- The *defiance* of the young is a bid to assert their individuality.

Anxiety

syn – Restlessness, apprehension, foreboding, worry, concern, misgiving, uneasiness, disquiet.

eg.

- There was *restlessness* in the audience when there was a delay in the proceedings.
- Anuradha had *misgivings* about the boy even before she learnt that he had a criminal record.

ant – Assurance, calmness, composure, confidence, ease, security, equanimity.

eg.

- The minister gave *assurance* to his constituency that he would try his best to improve the conditions of his people.
- Geetika's *calmness* and *composure* is exemplary.

Apparent

syn – Clear, visible, obvious, evident, manifest, distinct, plain.

eg.

- In the hills, the night sky is so *clear* that the stars are *visible* to the naked eye.
- It was *obvious* to the rest of the group that the couple had had a fight.

ant – Hidden, behind, obscure, veiled, secret, covert, latent, marked.

eg.

- The terrorist hand *behind* the bomb blast was uncovered by the media.
- He was giving a *veiled* hint to his beloved for fear of rejection.

Appear

syn – Emerge, seem, arise, occur, offer, open, loom, visible, manifest, look, show.

eg.

- The hills *loomed* up ahead as we drove round the bend.

- With his path breaking new ideas, Ravi has *emerged* as the star of this campaign.

ant – Disappear, invisible, vanish, fade away, wane.

eg.

- The moon *disappeared* behind the clouds.
- Soon after the theft, the thief *vanished* from the scene of crime.

Appoint

Syn – Assign, designate, name, employ, select, choose, hire.

eg.

- Atul was *named* as a party to the new policy because he was present at the meeting.
- Constable Radheysham had been *assigned* to guard duty on the fateful night of the terrorist attack.

ant – Discharge, let go, fire, suspend, withdraw.

eg.

- Spiritual masters implore us to *let go* of our vices if we want to be happy.
- The president decided to *fire* the surplus staff.

Appreciation

syn – Love, regard, respect, gratitude, praise, admiration, approval.

eg.

- All religions preach *love* for humanity.
- The parents' *approval* meant a lot to the new couple.

ant – Hate, disrespect, criticism, disregard, condemnation, disapproval.

eg.

- The greatest *disrespect* one can show to one's host is by *criticizing* their arrangement.
- All religions *disapprove* the use of violence.

Appropriate

syn – Confiscate, suitable, fitting, apt, take, right, proper, allot, seize, correct.

eg.

- The action taken by the government seemed *appropriate* to address the problem.
- This government is not tolerant of the wrong-doers and will *confiscate* all the property of the criminals.

ant – Inappropriate, release, incorrect.

eg.

- The student offended the teacher by passing an *inappropriate* remark.
- The answer was *incorrect*, so Sudhir did not get any marks.

Arms

syn – Armament, arsenal, deterrent, munitions, ordnance, weapons.

- Our country's *armaments* include modern and well equipped planes, ships and tanks.
- In India it is illegal to carry *weapons* without a license.

Ascent

syn – Further, climb, rise, gradient, go forward, incline, slope, progress, proceed.

eg.

- The *climb* to the peak of the mountain top was arduous.

- His *ascent* on his company ladder was both swift and spectacular.

ant – Bend, descent, go backward, regress, recede.

eg.

- The government is being criticized for *going back* on its commitments.
- The *descent* of the mountain was trickier than its climb uphill.

Assert

syn – Declare, state, emphasize, avow, affirm, allege, aver, avouch, maintain.

eg.

- Sukhi *declared* himself fit to drive.

- The teacher underlined the keywords to *emphasize* them.

ant – Contradict, dispute, demur, refute.

eg.

- There is another school of thought which *contradicts* the impor-tance of milk in our diet.
- The *dispute* between the brothers was settled in court.

Assiduous

syn – Industrious, diligent, active, busy, persevering, laborious, zealous.

eg.

- Ants are the most *industrious* living creatures.

- Samarth is *diligent* and hardworking.

ant – Indolent, lazy, lethargic, slothful.

eg.

- My younger brother is so *lazy* that he needs someone to do everything for him.
- The *indolent* salesman was kicked out of the company.

Associate

syn – Connect, ally, band, combine, confidante, unite, fraternize, join, relate, link.

eg.

- The Metro *connects* the important suburbs with the main commercial areas of Delhi.

- His close *band* of friends was waiting for him on the rooftop.

ant – Disconnect, dissociate, separate, break apart, distance, detach.

eg.

- In India, there seems to be a *disconnect* between the ruling party's ideologies and actions, which is apparent to the educated masses.
- She tried to *dissociate* herself from her rough gang of friends.

Assure

syn – Ensure, guarantee, certify, uphold, encourage, pledge, promise, inform.

eg.

- The company has to *guarantee* a minimum sales target.
- He took the *pledge* as the President of the country.

ant – Imperil, unsettle, discourage, mislead, warn, jeopardize.

eg.

- Lack of law and order *imperils* the country.
- The media *misleads* the people by exaggerating facts.

Astonish

syn – Surprise, amaze, astound, startle, confound.

eg.

- People were *amazed* at the magicians' tricks.

- The final results *surprised* the masses.

ant – Forewarn, caution, warn.

eg.

- The doctor *forewarned* the patient's family about the side effects of the medication.
- The principal *cautioned* the parents against indulging their errant child.

Atrocious

syn – Hideous, flagrant, outrageous, heinous, nefarious, diabolical, monstrous.

eg.

- The *hideous* ogre looked so dreadful that the princess fainted on seeing him.

- The rapist was given life term for the *heinous* crime he had committed.

ant – Noble, excellent.

eg.

- The freedom fighters were so *noble* that they placed their motherland above themselves and their families.
- The girl was in *excellent* health.

Attack

syn – Assail, assault, besiege, bombard, charge, storm.

eg.

- The army picked seasoned veterans to *storm* the key enemy post.
- *Besieged* with fear and insecurity, he decided to relocate and start afresh.

Ant – Aid, protect, uphold.

eg.

- The minister announced financial *aid* to the drought stricken areas.

- The army *upholds* values like loyalty, sincerity and discipline.

Attend

syn – Accompany, serve, guard, watch, escort, frequent, follow, listen, hear, wait, minister.

eg.

- The matron *accompanied* the young girl to the doctor.
- The policemen stood *guard* over the king's treasure.

ant – Desert, ignore, leave, disregard, overlook.

eg.

- The soldier *deserted* his post for a few minutes, and the enemy took advantage of it to enter the country.
- Radhika was hurt when she was *ignored* by her friends.

Attempt

syn – Effort, go, try, challenge, endeavor, crack, assay, aggression, assault.

eg.

- The fire fighters made an *effort* to climb the fire exit and enter the house.

- Shyam's *endeavor* to fix the model was appreciated by his teachers.

Attention

syn – Care, study, notice, thought, awareness, heed, regard, notice.

eg.

- The student brought the bad behavior of his friend to the teacher's *notice.*
- It is important to *heed* the feelings of other family members before taking any major decisions.

ant – Absence, distraction, remission.

eg.

- Rajiv's *absence* was greatly felt by his friends at te party.
- Television and computer cause unwanted *distraction* to a student.

Attest

syn – Show, testify, certify, vouch, authenticate, demonstrate, confirm, corroborate, indicate, mark, verify, argue.

eg.

- The witness *confirmed* that the suspect had left the house after the crime had been committed.
- The lawyer *argued* the case pleading for his client's innocence.

Attract

syn – Draw, charm, entice, tempt, decoy, enamor, captivate, magnetize, fascinate, pull.

eg.

- The little child's *charming* smile can *draw* strangers to her.
- Hitler's speeches were such that he could *captivate* a diverse audience with his oratory.

ant – Antagonize, repel, rile, irritate, annoy, exasperate.

eg.

- I get *repelled* by sly and mean people.
- The man's persistence *annoyed* the girl no end.

Attribute

syn – Quality, characteristic, trait, feature, point, aspect, ascribe, assign, credit, impute, refer, quality, property.

eg.

- The *trait* one associates the most with dogs is loyalty.
- The predominant *feature* of gypsy's is their nomadic life.

Attune

syn – Standardize, adjust, regulate, fix, set, integrate.

eg.

- The students took some time to *adjust* to the foreign accent of their new teacher.
- The junior officer was asked to *regulate* the timings of the battalion.

ant – Discordant.

eg.

- The out of tune guitar was the only *discordant* note in the entire orchestra.

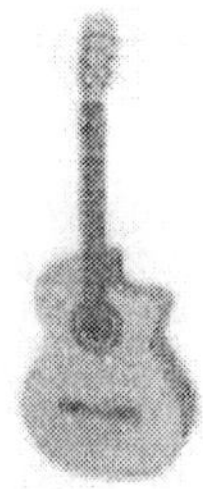

Auspicious

syn – Successful, hopeful, favorable, propitious, fortunate, lucky.

eg.

- The conservative parents enquired about the *favorable* dates from the priest to fix the marriage date.
- The businessman looked for a *propitious* date to start his new business.

ant – Despairing, inauspicious, ominous, unfortunate, unlucky, luckless, ill-fated.

eg.

- The *ill-fated* Titanic ship sank with all the passengers.

- The situation is *unfortunate,* and the government will have to help the needy farmers.

Authoritarian

Syn – Autocratic, despotic, dictatorial, fascist, totalitarian, tyrannical.

eg.

- Cromwell was certainly less *dictatorial* than many of his predecessors.
- Hitler's government was so *despotic* that the citizens could be shot without a trial.

Ant - Constitutional, compliant, democratic, lenient, liberal.

eg.

- The Indian government is one of the finest examples of a functional *democratic* government in the world.
- The new headmistress is quite *lenient* about assignments.

Authority

syn – Power, right, jurisdiction, influence, weight, prestige, title, control, command, sway, rule.

eg.

- There is a saying that *power* corrupts a man and absolute *power* corrupts absolutely.
- In Russia, the government *rules* the masses by *controlling* their economic and social activities.

ant – Submission, obedience, surrender, subjection, capitulation, slavery.

eg.

- The last date for *submission* of papers is 10th of Jan.'09.
- Alexander's army decided to *surrender* to the enemy.

Authentic

syn – Genuine, real, valid, bona fide, pure, true, uncorrupted.

eg.

- This shop supplies *genuine* artifacts.
- The police verified that the doctor had *bona fide* credentials.

ant – Spurious, adulterated, superficial.

eg.

- Many men died after consuming *spurious* liquor.
- The shopkeeper was fined for selling *adulterated* pulses.

Autocrat

syn – Dictator, tyrant, despot, authoritarian.

eg.

- Hitler was a *dictator* feared by the masses.
- The *tyrant* controls the masses, but he can never win their hearts.

ant – Democrat, benevolent.

eg.

- The *benevolent* patriarch was loved by all.
- The *democrat* leads the democratic country by taking into account the wishes and welfare of the people.

Auxiliary

syn – Supplementary, secondary, supporting, ancillary, subsidiary, contributory.

eg.

- The *ancillary* parts of the alloy wheel are difficult to source in the local market.

- The assistant's main task is to *supplement* the superior's duties.

ant – Opponent, essential.

eg.

- The secretary's *opponent* tried to pull him down by referring to a scandal from his past.
- The motor is an *essential* part of this device, and it will not function if the motor is not in working condition.

Avail

syn – Benefit, advantage, reward, gain, blessing, boon, favor, gain, profit, account, use, utility, serve.

eg.

- The company has offered an employee *benefit* plan to the senior management.
- The police has announced a *reward* for any information about the dacoit.

Aver

syn – Avow, state, claim, affirm, declare, profess, contend, say.

eg.

- "All those who are here for the service may proceed to the church," the minister *declared.*

- Rishi *claimed* that the car had rushed headlong into him.

Aversion

syn – Distaste, hate, dislike, loathing, repugnance, abomination, revulsion, anathema.

eg.

- He looked at the ill dressed tramp with *distaste.*
- She looked at the dead bird with revulsion.

ant – Admiration, adoration, approval, appreciation, wonder, awe.

eg.

- The teacher nodded his head in *approval* at the student's answer.
- The boys looked at the majestic sunset in silent *awe.*

Avoid

syn – Shun, evade, keep away from, circumvent, eschew, dodge, forbear, escape.

eg.

- He makes a conscious effort to *keep away from* conflicts and controversies.
- The minister tried to *dodge* the questions put up by the press.

ant – Catch, pursue, solicit, encounter.

eg.

- The hunters tried to *catch* the elephant.
- His *encounter* with the monkey herd left him quaking.

Award

syn – Bounty, honor, premium, prize.

eg.

- The robbers divided the *bounty* amongst themselves.
- He was awarded the highest state *honor* for bravery.

ant – Forfeit, penalty.

eg.

- The whole team had to pay the *penalty* for one player's misdemeanor.
- The government has decided to *forfeit* his award money.

Aware

syn – Alert, conscious, attentive, cognizant, responsive, informed, mindful.

eg.

- The patient was *conscious* when the surgery was performed.
- The student was quite *attentive* in the class.

ant – Unaware, heedless, ignorant, innocent.

eg.

- Sruti was *unaware* of the consequences of her action.
- Theresa was *ignorant* of the fact that Arvind had wiped her account clean.

Awe

syn – Fear, reverence, trepidation, wonder, veneration.

eg.

- The deer looked with *fear* at the hunter.

- The little children looked with *wonder* at the trapeze artist performing at the circus.

ant – Contempt, disregard, disdain, disrespect, scorn, derision.

eg.

- The king looked with *contempt* at the traitor.
- The teacher was unhappy with the *disrespect* shown by the students.

Awful

syn – Dreadful, appalling, dire, terrible, unpleasant, frightful, shocking, extremely, very, greatly.

eg.

- The train accident was an *appalling* sight.
- I was quite shaken up by the *terrible* experience.

ant – Appealing, pleasing, attractive, engaging, agreeable.

eg.

- The young recruit had an *attractive* personality.
- The farm fresh red apples looked *appealing* to the young child.

Awkward

syn – Unskillful, uncouth, ill-at-ease, uncomfortable, rough, bungling, maladroit, clumsy, gauche, gawky, coarse, ponderous, heavy handed.

eg.

- The lawyer's *unskillful* handling of the case landed Manmohan in jail.
- Raghavendra is so *uncouth* that the rest of the boys have started avoiding him.

ant – Skilful, dexterous, elegant, adroit, sophisticated, clever.

eg.

- Sumit's *skillful* handling of the project earned him the highest marks.
- The young girl was *dexterous* in her handling of the bow and arrow.

Awry

syn – Amiss, sour, wrong, astray, skewed, askew, out of kilter, twisted, off-center, off beam, crooked.

eg.

- The painting on the wall was *askew* and the carpenter was called to fix it.
- The dentist saw Sana's *crooked* teeth and advised braces.

ant – Usual, correct, accurate.

eg.

- The lawyer sat at his *usual* place in the restaurant.
- The engineer wrote down the *accurate* measurements of the bridge.

Axiom

syn – Maxim, adage, truism, saying, principle.

eg.

- 'Honesty is the best policy' is a good *adage* to live by.
- A *saying* condenses a long message in one sentence.

Ax

syn – Discharge, dismissal, terminate, boot, sack, fire, hatchet.

eg.

- The manager issued the *dismissal* orders of the errant clerk.
- When the new management took over, the old employees feared that they might get the *boot*.

B

Babble

Syn – Jabber, chatter, prattle, jibber, blather, chat, tattle, small talk.

eg.

- The children *chattered* non stop in the bus all the way to the picnic spot.

- The agent made *small talk* with the lawyer till his protégé arrived.

Ant – Quiet, silent.

eg.

- The patient's family sat *quietly* as he was wheeled into the operation theatre.
- The audience became *silent* as soon as the performer came on stage.

Baby

Syn – Infant, tot, toddler, babe, child, kid, newborn.

eg.

- Justine's second *child* was born when she lived in Bangalore.
- The *newborn* let out a lusty cry to announce his arrival.

Ant - Adult, mature, grown up.

eg.

- Jacky felt he was *mature* enough to handle his own problems.

- He had lived most of his *adult* life in Mumbai.

Back

Syn – Rear, reverse, recede, backtrack, retreat, attest, confirm, corroborate, validate, endorse, sponsor, support, uphold.

eg.

- The machinery was loaded in the *rear* of the truck.
- The students *supported* the idea that ragging should be banned in their college.

Ant – Front, precede, face.

eg.

- His reputation *precedes* him.
- The captain of the school team stood in the *front* to welcome the guest team.

Backward

Syn – Rearward, behind, primitive, underdeveloped.

eg.

- Some tribal areas in India are still quite *primitive.*
- The rural area looked *underdeveloped* but had immense potential.

Ant – Willing, ahead, advancing, forward.

eg.

- The army marched *forward* at the sound of the bugle.
- On seeing the *advancing* swarm of locusts, the farmer sent out the distress call to the neighboring villages.

Bad

Syn – Evil, disagreeable, awful, terrible, objectionable, noxious, depraved, corrupt, immoral, sinful, vile, mean, ghastly, horrific, inferior.

eg.

- The *evil* stepmother looked at the hapless princess and smiled.
- The *corrupt* police officer was sentenced to a six year jail term.

Ant – Good, moral, superior, fine, excellent, virtuous, desirable.

eg.

- The people adored their *virtuous* queen.
- The old man was in *excellent* health.

Badger

Syn – Bait, heckle, pester, hassle, harass, plague, taunt, needle, rile, harry.

eg.

- The little kid *pestered* his father to buy him a new toy.
- The salesman looked quite *hassled* by the lady's questions.

Badinage

Syn – Banter, chaff, raillery, taunt, ribbing, jest.

eg.

- The parents enjoyed the *banter* between their children.
- Vaibhav hid his sister's books in *jest*, but he was worried when he couldn't find them later.

Bag

Syn – Container, carrier, shopping bag, sack, handbag, purse.

eg.

- Surbhi bought an elegant *handbag* from the shopping arcade.

- The little boy dragged the heavy *shopping bag* behind him

Balance

Syn – Equilibrium, adjust, poise, stability, pit, steadiness, proportion, weight.

eg.

- He *adjusted* the volume of the music system when his sister complained that she was getting disturbed.
- A working woman has a tough time trying to *balance* home and career.

Ant – Over-balance, tilt, slant, tip, upset.

eg.

- The cart *tilted* on the uneven road and then overturned.
- The contestant's impressive speech *tipped* the scales in his favor.

Balderdash

Syn – Nonsense, drivel, rubbish, baloney, garbage, tripe.

eg.

- The senseless *drivel* of the girls infuriated him.
- The news channel was infamous for sensationalizing *tripe*.

Ant - Common sense, logic, sagacity, wisdom.

eg.

- The *sagacity* of the preacher's advice stuck home with most of the people.
- The kid's behavior defied all *logic*.

Balm

Syn – Allay, lull, quiet, settle, salve, ointment, comfort, relief, solace.

eg.

- The soothing music worked like a *balm* for her distraught nerves.
- After his wife left him, Suresh sought *solace* in his friend's company.

Ant – Wound, aggravate, injure, hurt.

eg.

- Mira's angry words *aggravated* the situation.
- The *wounded* animal lay unattended by the roadside.

Ban

Syn – Bar, prohibit, veto, outlaw, proscribe, disallow, interdict.

eg.

- Smoking is *prohibited* in the office building.
- The police seized his passport and *barred* him from leaving the country.

Ant - Allow, permit, agree, consent.

eg.

- Mother *agreed* to let us go for the camp.

- Kanya **eg.**was *permitted* by the doctor to resume her normal routine.

Banal

Syn – Inane, insipid, commonplace, trite, prosaic, ordinary, dull, boring.

eg.

- The *inane* party conversation made him feel so bored that he kept yawning again and again.
- The young bride found the early days of her marriage *dull* and *boring*.

Ant – Original, genuine, meaningful.

eg.

- The *original* work by this artist is in the country's best museum, the rest are copies.

- The treatise gives a *meaningful* insight into the laws of physics.

Bankrupt

Syn – Penniless, broke, bust, insolvent, ruined, indigent, destitute.

eg.

- The young *penniless* student gate crashed the wedding to enjoy a hearty meal.
- After he declared himself *insolvent*, his property was auctioned to pay his debts.

Ant – Solvent, credit-worthy, well-off, prosperous, rich.

eg.

- It is always profitable to buy the shares of a

company which strong and *solvent*.
- Aurangzeb Road is one of the best addresses, and its residents are some of the most *prosperous* and *rich* people of Delhi.

Bare

Syn – Naked, nude, exposed, uncovered, undressed, unclothed, stripped.

eg.
- She felt the sun warm on her *naked* arms.
- The newspaper *exposed* the minister's involvement in the scam.

Ant - Covered, clothed, dressed.

eg.
- The girls were *dressed* in formal attire for their school party.
- In conservative Muslim countries, women have to be *covered* from head to toe.

Bargain

Syn – Deal, inexpensive, haggle, barter, negotiate, transaction, agreement.

eg.
- The dishonest officer was caught trying to strike a *deal* with the corrupt builder.
- The lady tried her best to *haggle* with the stubborn shopkeeper, but was unsuccessful.

Ant – Account, rip-off, payment, expensive, quittance.

eg.
- The new showroom in our colony is a *rip-off* and quotes prices which are much higher than any where else.
- The client presented Suhani with an *expensive* gift to express her gratitude.

Barrier

Syn – Fence, wall, blockade, barricade, obstruction, difficulty, obstacle.

eg.
- The fans of the star were kept back behind *barricades*.

- Crowds burst through the *barriers* and ran onto the pitch.

Base

Syn – Corrupt, shameful, mean, sordid, low, dishonorable, vile, bottom, foot, pedestal.

eg.

- The policeman was shocked to hear the dalit woman's *sordid* tale.
- The mountain climbers decided to assemble at the foot of the mountain before proceeding together.

Ant – Above-board, pure, honored, esteemed, noble, exalted, lofty, top, peak, crest.

eg.

- The freedom fighters are *honored* for their selfless service to their country.
- Anand Bazaar Patrika is one of the oldest and *esteemed* dailies of northern India.

Battle

Syn – Fight, encounter, skirmish, clash, combat, scuffle.

eg.

- The *clash* between the two ethnic groups was instigated by the vested interests of the politicians.
- The dreaded terrorist was shot dead in a police *encounter*.

Ant - Peace, harmony.

eg.

- Forgiveness is the only way to attain *peace*.
- There was *harmony* among the different tribes living together in the jungles.

Bawdy

Syn – Coarse, vulgar, rude, lewd.

eg.

- We went to see a play, but it's language was so *vulgar* that we left after a couple of minutes.
- The rustic humor of the country bumpkin was quite *coarse* and out of place.

Ant - Refined, elegant, sophisticated.

eg.

- The young lady looked quite *elegant* in a sari.

- It was shocking to see the *sophisticated* woman hurling abuses at her servant.

Beat

Syn – Hit, strike, bang, hammer, thrash.

eg.

- The batsman *hit* the ball straight to the boundary.

- The little boy *hammered* on the door.

Bend

Syn – Bow, submit, stoop, curve, turn, yield, crook, twist, condescend, incline.

eg.

- Mahima *bowed* before her grandmother's wishes and agreed to marry Mohan.
- The driver did not slow down on the blind *curve* and met with an accident.

Ant – Stiffen, stand, straighten, advance, rise.

eg.

- Chetan tried to *straighten* the record by talking about his side of the story to the media.

- Indira was awestruck to see the sun *rise* from amor g the snow capped mountain peaks.

Before

Syn – Precede, earlier, ahead, prior to, in front of, previous to, formerly, already, above.

eg.

- The director asked the board members if they wanted to go *ahead* with the new project.
- Arvind quoted a passage from Hamlet, the famous play of Shakespeare, *before* starting his speech.

Ant – Succeeding, after, behind, later, following, subsequently, afterwards.

eg.

- The minister addressed the congregation *after* the family members had paid their tributes to the deceased.
- The little boy trailed *behind* his mother.

Beginning

Syn – **Start**, commencement, opening, launch, creation.

eg.

- The program is going to *start* any minute.
- The star was invited for the *opening* of Ritu's new boutique.

Ant - **End**, termination, ending, finish, conclusion.

eg.

- The author was struggling to give an appropriate *ending* of his latest novel.
- The teacher asked us to sum up the essay in the last paragraph or the *conclusion*.

Behind

Syn – Rear, after, following, last, bottom, back.

eg.

- The months *following* the traumatic accident

were the worst for Vishesh.

- Shobha's brother was determined to find the truth *behind* the mystery of her disappearance.

Ant - Front, leading.

eg.

- He drove straight into the car in *front*.
- The Deccan Chargers were *leading* the cricket series.

Belief

Syn – Trust, credit, faith, conviction, opinion, view, mind, idea.

eg.

- The masses do not *trust* those politicians who make promises at the time of elections and later forget them.
- *Faith* and *conviction* can see you through the toughest times.

Ant – Distrust, whim, misgiving, discredit, suspicion, doubt, disbelief.

eg.

- *Distrust* in any relationship takes an instant, whereas trust takes a long time to grow.
- The whole household danced to the *whims* and fancies of the old woman

Beneath

Syn – Below, underneath, under, down, lower than.

eg.

- The footnotes *below* the treatise explained all its difficult terms.
- The treasure hunters hoped they would be able to find the treasure hidden *under* the sea.

Ant – Up, overhead, above, high.

eg.

- The hot air balloon rose *high above* the ground and soon was out of sight.
- The children stood and watched the airplane flying *overhead*.

Benefit

Syn – Profit, gain, favor, advantage, avail, service, boon.

eg.

- The company showed *profit* for the year ending 2009.
- The teacher took *advantage* of the extra working day and finished the course.

Ant – Harm, loss, damage, disadvantage, injury, calamity.

eg.

- The Sharma's garment unit showed a *loss* of Rs. 5, 00,000 in the last accounting year.
- The victim's family claimed *damages* from the car driver.

Benevolence

Syn – God's grace, selflessness, generosity, charity, humanity, fellow feeling, brotherly love, kindness, mercy, piety, compassion, munificence.

eg.

- Karna's *generosity* is legendary.
- Little Pooja's *kindness* towards the stray cat was appreciated by her parents.

Ant – Ill-nature, spite, cruelty, inhumanity, enmity, hate, malice, venom, churlishness, malevolence.

eg.

- The Verma's gardener was fired after he showed *cruelty* to the poor little boy
- War just perpetrates *malice* and *inhumanity,* and doesn't solve anything.

Bewilder

Syn – Problem, confuse, baffle, bamboozle, poser, puzzle, perplex, mystery, enigma.

eg.

- The difficult algebra problem *baffled* the professor.
- The *mystery* of the Hingorani's missing jewelry was solved by the vigilant detective.

Ant – Enlighten, teach, illuminate, inform, edify, instruct.

eg.

- Buddha and the other *enlightened* teachers are born to lead and guide the rest of us.
- The students did not let the new teacher *teach* on the first day.

Best

Syn – Greatest, paramount, finest, superlative, excellent.

eg.

- Joshi's proposal was *excellent,* and the management decided to implement it
- Sania Mirza is one of the *finest* tennis players in the world.

Ant - Worst, bad, awful, horrible, terrible.

eg.

- My teacher was in a very *awful* mood today.
- The pudding tasted *terrible*.

Between

Syn – Amid, among, linking, involving.

eg.

- The ball rolled *between* his feet.
- He divided his money equally *among* his children.

Beyond

Syn – Across, farther, yonder, ahead of, outside, afar, over.

eg.

- In the obstacle race, Sudhir was way *ahead of* his other classmates.
- The bored student looked *outside* the window while the teacher taught.

Ant – Adjacent, beside, along, next, near, close.

eg.

- The two intern doctors decided to take *adjacent* cabins in the hospital.
- Madan parked his car *next* to his neighbor's swanky new car.

Beyond

Syn – Further, past, outside, afar, ahead of.

eg.

- With inflation, even daily necessities are now *beyond* the reach of the common man.
- The kids raced on *ahead* while we strolled in the park.

Ant - Within, inside, in.

eg.

- True beauty lies *within*.
- Mother asked the gentleman to come *in*.

Binding

Syn – Obligatory, contract, compulsory, required, holding, restraining, stringent, valid.

eg.

- The court issued a *restraining* order against the stalker.
- The starlet's *contract* forbade her to talk to the media about her debut movie.

Ant – Optional, voluntary, elective, discretional.

eg.

- Arhaan excelled in his *elective* subjects, but did not do so well in the compulsory subjects.
- The judge suggested that criminals should be given the *option* of paying the fine or putting in a fixed number of hours in social service.

Bind

Syn – Attach, connect, join, combine, tie, fasten.

eg.

- Their shared experiences in the war helped to *bind* the two communities together.
- The edges of the baby's blanket were *tied* with ribbons.

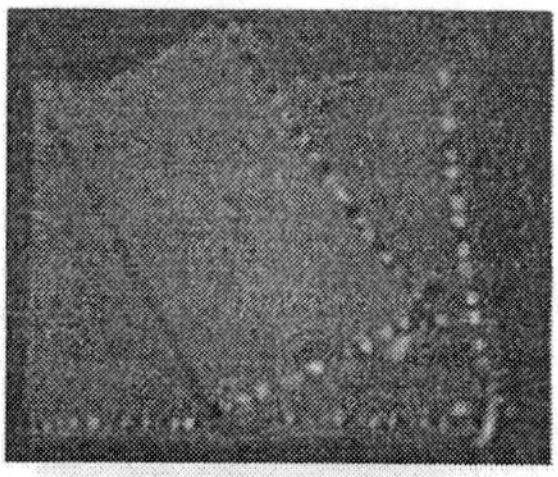

Ant - Unbind, loosen, release, liberate, unshackle, untie.

eg.

- The little boy *released* the bird from its cage.
- When Jayesh got marr-

ied, his mother was advised by well-meaning relatives to *untie* the umbilical cord.

Birth

Syn – Origin, delivery, dawn, beginning, creation, genesis.

eg.

- The visitors were awestruck when they saw the beautiful sunlit sky at *dawn*.
- Darwin's theory about the *origin* of man has been disputed by different scientists.

Ant – End, finish, close, death, conclusion.

eg.

- The athlete was *close* to the *finish* line when he slipped and fell.
- The patient's family knew that his *end* was near.

Bitter

Syn – Sad, acrid, intense, pungent, harsh, sour, severe.

eg.

- The *acrid* fumes brought tears to his eyes.
- Santya felt *sad* after the *bitter* fight with her best friend.

Ant – Mild, sweet, pleasant, genial, light.

eg.

- The *mild* mannered old gentleman was liked by all the neighbors.
- The *genial* host beamed amicably at all the guests.

Blame

Syn – Criticism, responsibility, reproach, censure, fault, rebuke, guilt.

eg.

- Theresa *rebuked* her you-nger brother for bunk-ing school.
- My dog's eyes were full of *reproach* when I showed him four biscuits, but gave him only three.

Ant – Praise, appreciation, applaud, honor, admire, commend, approval, exhort, extol.

eg.

- Bina's short dress did not meet with her mother's *approval*.
- We *admire* good leaders for their selfless contribution to the country and countrymen.

Blessing

Syn – Good wishes, prayer, sanction, praise, thanks, consecration.

eg.

- The priest *thanked* the congregation for being so committed and receptive.
- The *good wishes* of family and friends led to Randhir's speedy recovery.

Ant – Bad wishes, curse, evil thought.

eg.

- Illiteracy is the biggest *curse* of any developed country.
- Bhram believed that the fire in his factory was the result of *bad wishes* of his relatives.

Blind

Syn – Sightless, window shade, screen, canopy, shade, visor.

eg.

- Milton was almost *blind* when he composed his greatest epics - Paradise Lost and Paradise Regained.
- The *blinds* were drawn to protect the furniture from the sun.

Ant - Sight, vision.

eg.

- My father's *sight* is quite good for his age.
- Jawaharlal Nehru had a vision of a modern and progressive India.

Bliss

Syn – Joy, pleasure, happiness, ecstasy, delight, rapture.

eg.

- I was happy to see the *delight* on the child's face when I gave him the ball he'd been eyeing for a long time.
- Wordsworth, the famous poet, has written a poem describing the beauty of a rainbow and how much *pleasure* it gave him.

Ant – Sorrow, sadness, pain, distress, anguish, agony, dejection.

eg.

- I saw the *sorrow* on my nephew's face when he

saw that his bird had died.

- Yuvi did not want to add to his friend's *anguish* by telling him that the accident was his mistake, so he kept quiet.

Block

Syn – Chunk, lump, slab, wedge, obstruct, hinder, impede, thwart.

eg.

- The huge building across the street *blocked* our view of the sea.

- The stone *slab* looked quite ugly in the kitchen.

Ant - Unblock, clear, free, unclog, clean out.

eg.

- The police *cleared* the way for the celebrity to pass.
- The plumber *unclogged* the drain pipes.

Blow

Syn – Gust, waft, puff, bluster, propel, drive, carry.

eg.

- He *blew* the smoke rings right in my face.
- The *gust* of wind banged the door shut.

Blue

Syn – Azure, cobalt, sapphire, navy, depressed, down.

eg.

- You can go *blue* in the face denying the affair, but no one is going to believe you.
- The young man was feeling *depressed* after losing his job.

Ant - Happy, cheerful.

eg.

- The little boy was *happy* to be home again.
- Maria is a *cheerful* girl.

Blunt

Syn – Direct, rounded, intensive, dull, undiplomatic.

eg.

- The minister's *undiplomatic* answers spelt trouble for his party.

- The victim had been killed with a *rounded* club.

Ant – Diplomatic, sensitive, sharp, sophisticated.

eg.

- The *diplomatic* ties between the two countries were severed when the cricket star was shot down during a match.
- The boy's mother was uneducated, but had a *sharp* mind.

Boiling

Syn – Hot, sweltering, scorching, roasting, steaming, torrid.

eg.

- "Can I open the door? It's *boiling* in here."
- The Censor Board asked the director to remove the *torrid* scenes from the movie.

Ant - Freezing, cold, icy, chilly, glacial.

eg.

- Alcohol has a lower *freezing* point than water.
- She gave the young man an *icy* stare.

Bond

Syn – Tie, link, attachment, connection, union, relationship, friendship, alliance.

- The emotional *bond* between a mother and her child does not get snapped with the umbilical cord.

- The Ullemas share a special *relationship* with the Mirzas.

Boom

Syn – Roar, bang, blast, thunder, growl, grumble, roll, rumble, prosper, thrive.

eg.

- The *roar* of the lion scared all the other animals in the jungle.

- My dog hid under the table when he heard the *bang* of the firecracker.

Ant – Bust, downfall.

eg.

- The recession has seen the smaller companies go *bust*.
- The *downfall* of the Roman Empire was brought about by weak kings and powerful ministers.

Boost

Syn – Encouragement, lift, aid, heighten, enhance, help, recommendation, hoist.

eg.

- Little Ayan needed no *encouragement* from his friends to climb the mango tree.
- The chief guest stood up as the captain stepped on the podium to *hoist* the flag.

Ant – Rebuke, discouragement, hindrance, censure, reproach, obstacle, rebuff.

eg.

- The teacher *rebuked* Shram for being late in the class.
- The *discouragement* from his teachers demoralized Ankit so much that he left the school.

Bore

Syn – Troublesome, tire, weary, irk, talker, nuisance, talkative, pest.

eg.

- Zafar was *irked* by the incessant chatter of the women in his office.
- Vinita is the most *talkative* girl in her class.

Ant – Thinker, entertainer, enlightened, amusing, listener.

eg.

- Aristotle was the foremost *thinker* of his times.

- The best way to show your friend that you care is to be an interested *listener*.

Borrow

Syn – Receive, appropriate, take, use, scrour ge, sponge, adapt, imitate, copy, pirate, adopt.

eg.

- Rishi had to *take* the gardener's tools to the shed before he left for work.
- The company had to *adopt* certain guidelines to streamline its working procedures.

Ant – Lend, advance, give, improve, make credit.

eg.

- The businessman agreed to *lend* money to his friend.
- The teacher decided to *give* assignment to the class for the holidays.

Boundary

Syn - Border, frontier, border line, edge, limit, margin, periphery.

eg.

- The Mississippi River forms a natural *boundary* between Iowa and Illinois.
- Modern India is witnessing a blurring of the *border line* between traditional values and modernity.

Ant - Core, nucleus, crux, centre, hub.

eg.

- Miraj handles the *core* group of clients himself.
- The hotel is right in the *centre* of the town.

Brace

Syn – Support, refresh, invigorate, prop, strengthen.

eg.

- A good mattress is as important to *strengthen* the back as a good exercise regimen.
- Pinki breathed in the fresh *invigorating* air of the hills and felt rejuvenated.

Ant – Weaken, degenerate, raze, knock, enfeeble.

eg.

- She heard Praveen's voice *weaken* with emotion when her son said 'Mama' for the first time.
- The fossils were discovered in a *degenerated* state.

Brave

Syn – Bold, courageous, dauntless, gallant, heroic, intrepid, plucky, undaunted, valiant, valorous.

eg.

- The *valiant* king faced the enemy heroically.
- The *bold* and *courageous* woman stood up to the terrorists and fought with them till the police came.

Ant – Afraid, cowardly, timid, weak, daunted, intimidated.

eg.

- Little Ryan is *afraid* of the dark.
- Akshar was *intimidated* by the tall menacing bodyguard of his girlfriend.

Breach

Syn – Rupture, opening, gap, fissure, violate, contravene, infringe, rift, falling out, chasm.

eg.

- The dentist advised that the *gap* between Vani's teeth could only be rectified with braces.
- The judge told the errant husband that his adulterous affair *violated* the trust between man and wife, and he would therefore have to pay a higher alimony.

Ant – Honor, observance, reconciliation, bridge.

eg.

- A gentleman will always *honor* his word.
- The judge said that it is always better for the couple to try *reconciliation* before seeking divorce.

Break

Syn – Interlude, intermission, interval, respite, pause, recess, smash, rupture, crack, split, shatter, sever.

eg.

- The children couldn't wait till the *intermission* to have popcorn, so Mahi got them just as the movie started.
- Arun's motorcycle banged into the speeding car and *shattered* its glass window.

Ant – Continuation, connection, mend, repair, fix, restore, revamp, darn, patch.

eg.

- The seamstress sat down to *mend* her mistress' gown.
- When Paul could not hear his sister's voice clearly, he knew it was time to *fix* his hearing aid.

Breed

Syn – Produce, reproduce, class, strain, raise, beget, conceive, train, hatch, incubate.

eg.

- All living beings *reproduce* their own kind.
- There is an old saying that 'Like *begets* liking'.

Ant – Destroy, slay, raze, murder, annihilate, sterile, fecund.

eg.

- In the terror attack, the big buildings adjoining the Capitol were *razed* to the ground.
- The rebels plotted to *slay* the dissident leader.

Breeze

Syn – Storm, waft, gust, zephyr, hurricane, wind, blast, gale, air, typhoon walkover, child's play.

eg.

- The warm *gust* of desert *wind* hit our faces as soon as we opened the car door.
- Working out the solution for the complex mathematical problem was *child's play* for Neelesh.

Ant – Lull, placidity, calm.

eg.

- There was stillness in the air, and my father told me that it was a *lull* before the storm.
- My English teacher has a *calm* and serene face.

Brevity

Syn – Concise, short, succinct, brief.

eg.

- The examiner asked us to keep our answers *concise* and to the point.
- The judge asked the lawyer to sum up the case in *short* highlighting only the important aspects.

Ant – Lengthy, cumbersome.

eg.

- The chief guest went on to give a *lengthy* speech and delayed the proceedings even further.
- The thesis work required *cumbersome* and arduous preparation.

Bright

Syn – Shining, quick-witted, intelligent, vivid, clear, luminous, resplendent, dazzling, sparkling.

eg.

- The evening sky was *resplendent* with stars.

- The little girl was sharp and *quick-witted*.

Ant – Dull, dim-witted, foolish, dark, ignorant, faint.

eg.

- The order had to be repeated a number of times before the *dim-witted* waiter got it right.

- The *faint* silhouette of the man in the dark looked like a tree.

Brisk

Syn – Quick, alert, industrious, fast, rapid, busy, lively, hurried, vigorous, prompt, energetic.

eg.

- The *fast* urban lifestyle is taking a toll on our health.
- The coach started the class after a *vigorous* exercise session.

Ant – Slow, lethargic, dull, lazy, indolent, inactive.

eg.

- The summer sun made us feel *lethargic* enough to want to take a nap.
- The hare and tortoise story proves the point that *slow* and steady wins the race.

Brusque

Syn – Discourteous, abrupt, rude, gruff, rough, curt

eg.

- Paul's tone was *curt* as he informed the board of directors that he was resigning from the post of the CEO.
- The old man's voice was *gruff* as he pointed out to the doctors that he was well enough to leave the hospital.

Ant – Courteous, smooth, polite, chivalrous, polished.

eg.

- The hotel manager turned down the offer *politely* to join the competitor.
- The host asked after each guest *courteously*.

Brutal

Syn – Inhuman, vicious, evil, wicked, vile, merciless, savage, pitiless, barbaric, cruel.

eg.

- The *inhuman* atrocities inflicted on the war prisoners stirred up activists all over the world.

- The fairy tales have made the *evil* step mother a metaphor for cruelty.

Ant – Humane, merciful, sympathetic, kind, compassionate, tender.

eg.

- Mother Teresa was a *kind* and *compassionate* woman.
- The psychologist tried a *humane* approach with the death row victim.

Build

Syn – Construct, erect, fabricate, make, put up, assemble, manufacture.

eg.

- The art director *erected* the set for the movie on the outskirts of the city.
- Raoul *assembled* the lego pieces and made the model of an airplane.

Ant – Destroy, devastate, raze, unmake.

eg.

- The builder decided to *raze* the house to the ground and make new apartments instead.
- The earthquake in Bhuj *destroyed* entire villages.

Bustle

Syn – Rustle, activity, flutter, flurry, hum, buzz, stir, fluster, ado.

eg.

- There was a *flurry* of *activity* in the college corridor as the principal entered.
- There was a *hum* of excitement as soon as the star entered the classroom.

Ant – Inertness, laziness, fatigue, lull, rest, passivity, dullness, delay, inaction.

eg.

- The doctor advised the patient to take a healthy diet and complete *rest* for the next one week.
- The announcer informed the passengers that the flights were going to be *delayed* even further.

Busy

Syn – Active, occupied, diligent, tiring, industrious, engrossed.

eg.

- It is very important for the retired people to

keep themselves *active* and *occupied*.

- Talbot wanted to relax at home after a *tiring* day at work, but his wife wanted to go out and party.

Ant – Indolent, idle, passive, sluggish, slothful, relaxed, inactive, lazy, unoccupied, inert.

eg.

- Sharman was furious to see his young son lying *inert* in front of the television the whole day long.
- The young working couple decided to stay indoors since they were feeling too *lazy* to step out.

C

Cab

Syn – Taxi, taxicab, yellow cab.

eg.

- I took a *cab* to the airport.

- Carriages pulled by horses were used like a *taxi* in the middle ages

Cabal

Syn – Group, unit, sect, faction, section, intrigue, plot.

eg.

- The members of the minority *sect* put up a demonstration to demand their rights.
- The *plot* to assassinate the king was uncovered by the police just in time.

Cabinet

Syn – Cupboard, dresser, group of ministers.

eg.

- The carpenter made the *cupboard* for my new room.
- The leader of the ruling party asked for a *cabinet* meeting to resolve the issue.

Cable

Syn – Wire, rope, line, lead, chain.

eg.

- The Residents' Association requested the government to substitute the overhead power *cables* with the underground ones.

- Shubhra asked her son to *chain* his bicycle to the fence.

Cackle

Syn – Laugh, hoot, screech, crow, guffaw.

eg.

- The *screech* of the wild birds made the jungle seem eerie.
- The announcement was met with loud *guffaws.*

Cadaver

Syn – Corpse, dead, dead body remains.

eg.

- The grieving family agreed to donate the *cadaver* to the medical school.

- The police found the *corpse* of the girl hidden in the shrubs.

Cache

Syn – Inventory, reserve, stash, reservoir, stock, store, supply.

eg.

- The manager informed his superior that they had enough *stock* to last them through the summers.
- In winters, squirrels dig into their *stash* of nuts collected during the summer season.

Cacophonous

Syn – Discordant, jarring, dissonant, harsh, out of tune.

eg.

- The sound of the machine cutting the glass was *jarring* on Subhadra's nerves.
- The guitar was *out of tune*, and the performance of the orchestra was ruined because of it.

Ant – Melodious, musical.

eg.

- The audience enjoyed listening to old Hindi songs in Asha's *melodious* voice.
- The *musical* evening held at the Old Fort in Delhi was appreciated by one and all.

Cadence

Syn – Tempo, pace, rhythm, beat, pulse, lilt, intonation.

eg.

- The *cadence* of my mother's voice told me that my brother was getting a yelling in the next room.
- Drums are basic to African *rhythm*.

Cage

Syn – Confine, enclose, pen, coop up, impound, shut in.

eg.

- The new bride hated being *confined* to her room every day.
- The children were *cooped up* in a small minivan and taken to the orphanage.

Cajole

Syn – Inveigle, coax, beguile, flatter, wheedle.

eg.

- The clerk tried to *flatter* his superior so he could get an extra day's leave.
- The wily courtesan tried to *wheedle* state secrets from the drunken minister.

Cake

Syn - Bar (used as 'a cake of soap), block, slab, lump, birthday cake.

eg.

- Punita decided to bake him a chocolate *cake* for his birthday.

- Our boots were *caked* with mud.

Calamity

Syn – Misery, distress, misfortune, mishap, trouble, catastrophe, affliction, disaster.

eg.

- After the devastating earthquake, the government announced aid for the *distressed*.
- *Misfortune* cannot be averted, but faith and rituals can help one to handle them better.

Ant – Prosperity, fortune, peace, affluence, opulence, joy, tranquility, happiness.

eg.

- In olden days India was termed as a 'golden sparrow' and the people here enjoyed both *peace* and *prosperity*.
- The mansion of the Malhotras displayed the *affluence* befitting his status as the richest man of the city.

Calculate

Syn – Reckon, gauge, determine, evaluate, count, assess, analyze, estimate, number, compute.

eg.

- The manager called his accountant to give an *estimate* of the profit for the current working year.
- According to the new education policy, the students are going to be *evaluated* right through the year.

Ant – Imagine, conjecture, surmise, suppose.

eg.

- It is difficult to *imagine* life without electricity.
- The detective's *conjecture* about the assailant's identity proved to be correct.

Call

Syn – Bid, yell, holler, whoop, come over, drop by, term, buzz, telephone, ring, recall, invite, summon, convene, muster, invoke.

eg.

- Kedar asked his mother if his friend could *come over* for dinner the following day.
- Mohit promised to give his parents a *buzz* as soon as he reached his college safely.

Calm

Syn – Pacify, tranquil, peaceful, hush, quiet, solace, mitigate, palliate, lull, composed, serene, cool, still.

eg.

- Our vacation in the *serene* mountain log cabin soothed our senses.
- The nanny tried to *pacify* the crying baby by rocking her back and forth.

Ant – Agitate, excite, perturb, crisis, disturb, fluster.

eg.

- The sight of the accident victims *perturbed* even the most stout hearted.
- The doctor warned the patient's family not to *disturb* or *excite* him unnecessarily.

Cancel

Syn – Destroy, abolish, call off, obliterate, stop, abandon, withdraw, nullify, invalidate, erase, blot out, efface.

eg.

- Raja Ram Mohan Roy was responsible for *abolishing* the practice of Sati.
- The court ruled that the earlier will would be *nullified,* and the recent one taken into consideration.

Ant – Establish, ratify, corroborate, substantiate, endorse, confirm.

eg.

- The police report pointed out that there was enough evidence to *corroborate* the witness' account.
- The medical report *confirmed* what the doctor had been suspecting all along.

Cantankerous

Syn – Crabby, cranky, ill-tempered, grumpy, snappy, grouchy, irascible, testy.

eg.

- The little boys were scared of the *crabby* old gentleman who lived close to the playing ground.
- Uma did not like her *grouchy* grandparents at all.

Ant – Agreeable, pleasant, charming, pleasing.

eg.

- Our new neighbors are *charming* and *pleasant* people.
- My English teacher has a very *pleasing* personality.

Capacity

Syn – Capability, ability, competence, aptitude, faculty, wit, skill, power, talent.

eg.

- Shubhi has the patience and *capability* to manage a class full of small children.

- One needs both *competence* and *skill* to be successful in one's career.

Ant – Incapability, inability, incompetence, ineptitude.

eg.

- Meera's parents were disappointed by her *inability* to clear the prelims.
- The manager was very annoyed by Sridhar's *incompetence*.

Capture

Syn – Arrest, seize, imprison, detain, incarcerate, jail, confine, snatch, catch, apprehend.

eg.

- The police *apprehended* the thief as he was about to flee the scene of crime.
- The customs *seized* the illegal goods brought into the country by the smuggler.

Ant – Liberate, release, unshackle, acquit, free, disengage.

eg.

- The little boy decided to *release* the bird from its cage.
- In order to concentrate on studies, one must *disengage* one's mind from any distractions.

Careful

Syn – Meticulous, cautious, wary, vigilant, alert, conscientious, scrupulous, watchful.

eg.

- Yogi's mother advised him to be *cautious* of pickpockets in the crowded mall.
- Shraddha is very *meticulous* in her work.

Ant – Negligent, apathetic, shoddy, lackadaisical, heedless, sloppy, careless, slipshod.

eg.

- The patient's family accused the doctors of being *negligent*.
- Araav's mother was very unhappy about his *shoddy* dressing style.

Carry

Syn – Bear, lug, bring, haul, cart, convey, clutch, take, transport, transmit.

eg.

- The porter *hauled* the big suitcase into the boot of the car.
- The police used helicopters to *transport* the paratroopers into enemy territory.

Ant – Leave, abandon, drop.

eg.

- The young mother decided to *leave* her job to attend to her home and children.
- The little girl *dropped* her heavy bag on the pavement.

Cast

Syn – Bent, bias, disposition, leaning, penchant, predilection, proclivity, propensity, tendency, expression (used as 'cast of countenance'), visage, throw (used as 'cast one's mind back'), sling, aim, direct, emit, radiate, shed, project, look, search.

eg.

- Manoj has a *penchant* for using long sentences in hi articles.
- Shubhra's *expression* changed when she realized that she had been caught cheating.

Ant – Keep, retain.

eg.

- Vijaya asked the shopkeeper to *keep* the change.
- The theatre manager advised the audience to *retain* their tickets till the time they left the premises.

Casualty

Syn – Mishap, incident, chance, calamity, misadventure, victim, injured person.

eg.

- The train *mishap* left the survivors in a state of shock.

- The government announced compensation for the families of the *victims* of the bomb blast.

Catastrophe

Syn – Misfortune, calamity, disaster, mishap, debacle, cataclysm.

eg.

- The article talked about the *misfortune* which

befell the rich industrialist's family.

- The stock market *debacle* has turned the fortunes of many upside down.

Ant – Blessing, boon, fortune.

eg.

- The couple told the doctor that it was a *blessing* to have a healthy child.
- The advanced technology is both a *boon* and a curse.

Catching

Syn – Infectious, communicable, contagious, transmissible.

eg.

- The school authorities have asked the parents to keep the children at home if they had any *contagious* disease.
- The swine flu scare was made worse by the fact that it is highly *infectious*.

Ant – Unpleasant, ugly, unattractive, revolting, loathsome, repellent, odious, disagreeable.

eg.

- The pile of garbage looked quite *unattractive* in the otherwise clean colony.
- The smelly beggar looked quite *revolting*.

Cause

Syn – Produce, bring about, origin, create, evoke, reason, grounds, source, basis, foundation.

eg.

- The new education minister promised to *bring about* the desired reforms.

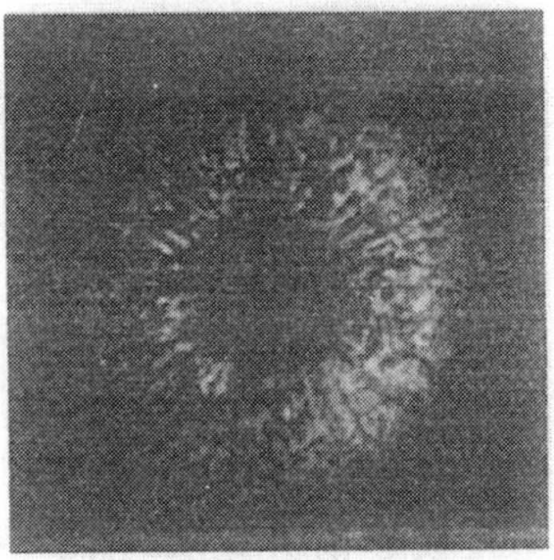

- The Big Bang Theory tells us about the *origin* of the universe.

Ant – Result, consequence, outcome, upshot, effect.

eg.

- The military had not estimated that the *outcome* of the nuclear bombs would be so devastating.
- Our school's principal praised the efforts of the faculty and students for getting such a spectacular academic *result*.

Cease

Syn – End, discontinue, halt, pause, stop, finish.

eg.

- The teacher asked the class to *finish* the work in silence.
- The director decided to *end* the discussion by quoting statistics to support his argument.

Ant – Start, continue, create, begin, carry on, pursue.

eg.

- The movie *started* on time.
- The professor told Anuj to *carry on* working sincerely if he wanted a promotion.

Cede

Syn – Abandon, abdicate, yield, concede, give up, hand over, relinquish, resign, surrender, waive, assign.

eg.

- The old monarch decided it was time to *relinquish* the throne and named his heir apparent.
- The CEO had to *resign* from his post in the face of controversy.

Ant – Keep, retain.

eg.

- When everyone around her was screaming, Uma was sensible enough to *keep* her cool.
- The manager considered himself lucky that he could *retain* his post despite the economic depression.

Celebrated

Syn – Notable, famous, renowned, distinguished, eminent, illustrious, noted.

eg.

- The scientist was *renowned* for his path breaking discovery in the field of medicine.
- The chief guest of our school function was the *eminent* author, Shobha De.

Ant – Unnoticed, undistinguished, unknown, nameless.

eg.

- Despite working in the same company for a number of years, Joe was relatively *unknown*.
- The quiet and unassuming student was *unnoticed* by the teachers till he won the state championship.

Censorship

Syn – Disapproval, criticism, restriction, control, blame.

eg.

- It takes more strength of character to deal with *criticism* than handle praise.
- Mini's small dress met with her parents' *disapproval*.

Ant – Approval, commendation, appreciation, freedom.

eg.

- Democracy allows *freedom* of the media, but it should not be misused.
- Manish was extremely happy when he got a letter of *commendation* from his college.

Center

Syn – Core, middle, hub, axis, midst, heart.

eg.

- In the 70s, Connaught Place used to be the *hub* of all commercial and political activity in Delhi.
- I live in the suburbs and my office is in the *heart* of the city.

Ant – Remote, boundary, edge, perimeter.

eg.

- Our gardener has put a flowering creeper on the *boundary* wall of our garden.

- The engineer calculated the cost of covering the *perimeter* wall of the house with two strings of light.

Certain

Syn – Positive, assured, definite, indisputable, confident, firm, sure, actual, unequivocal, incontestable.

eg.

- The young contestant was *confident* of winning the title.
- The blue chip companies guarantee *assured* returns.

Ant – Doubtful, indefinite, disputable, uncertain, ambiguous, equivocal.

eg.

- It is *doubtful* if the teacher will agree to a re-evaluation of the test paper.
- Purab's program was *uncertain*, so mother asked him to call her and let her know.

Change

Syn – Veer, alter, shift, vary, diversify, adjust, amend, modify, convert, transfigure, transform, transmute.

eg.

- The government announced that the foreign policy would be *modified* very soon.
- The company has decided to *diversify* into associated products.

Ant – Hold fast, clinch, maintain, fix, sustain, stabilize, stand.

eg.

- The railing was fixed to the *adjoining* wall.

- The government announced new measures to *stabilize* the economy.

Chaos

Syn – Disorder, confusion, bedlam, pandemonium, anarchy, disarray, commotion.

eg.

- There was *commotion* in the house of speakers as some members objected to the motion suggested by the opposition party.
- The whole room was in *disarray* after the toddlers' party got over.

Ant – Order, organized, government.

eg.

- The police commissioner conveyed his concern about *organized* crime in the city.
- The judge asked for *order* to be maintained in the courtroom.

Charity

Syn – Kindness, generosity, philanthropy, almsgiving, aid, donation, benevolence.

eg.

- All religions preach the values of *kindness* and *generosity*.
- The big businessman was known for his *philanthropy*.

Ant – Meanness, greed, avarice, selfishness.

eg.

- Abhay's *meanness* was well known in his friends' circle.
- There is a difference between need and *greed*, and we need to understand it well.

Change

Syn – Alter, exchange, modify, vary, adjust, amend, substitute, transform, convert, transmute.

eg.

- The dietician asked Dolly to *modify* her diet if she wanted to lose weight.
- My mother asked my brother to *amend* his unruly ways.

Ant – Sustain, stabilize.

eg.

- The roots of trees reach for water and *sustain* it.

- The investors waited for the economy to *stabilize* before investing in stocks and shares.

Charisma

Syn – Allure, appeal, charm, pull, draw, magnetism.

eg.

- *Charm* sits like a bloom on a woman; if she has it, nothing else matters, if she doesn't, it doesn't matter what else she has.

- The actor exuded a raw cowboy *appeal*.

Ant – Ugliness, repulsiveness.

eg.

- The *repulsiveness* of the creepy snakes in the cage sent a tingle up my spine.

- The *ugliness* of her burnt face was well compensated by her sweet and serene expression.

Charge

Syn – Accuse, indict, allege, attack, onslaught, command (used as 'take charge'), instruct, trust (used as 'placed in charge'), cost, expense, price, sum.

eg.

- The suspect was *accused* of theft and attempt to murder.
- The *cost* of living is at an all-time high today.

Chart

Syn – Table, tabulation, blueprint, design, frame, plan, project, work out (used as 'chart out a course of action')

eg.

- The professor drew a *table* on the blackboard to explain the correlation between stock prices and inflation.
- The architect submitted the *blueprint* of his *design* to the CEO of the company.

Chase

Syn – Follow, hunt, pursue, hound, trail, track.

eg.

- The policeman *followed* the car which was reported to be carrying narcotics.
- The media *hounded* the star till he gave them a statement.

Ant – Forgo, renounce, withdraw, leave, abandon, forsake.

eg.

- Lord Ram *renounced* the throne and went to the forest to fulfill his father's promise.
- The unwed mother decided to *abandon* her newborn baby.

Cheap

Syn – Worthless, inferior, mean, low priced, discounted, inexpensive, common, paltry, contemptible, despicable, shameful.

eg.

- Priya bought some *inexpensive* but beautiful bedcovers from the wholesale market.

- The old watch was *worthless*, but Dad refused to part with it.

Ant – Worthy, noble, lofty, honorable, eminent, expensive, dear, costly, superior.

eg.

- With the new Bose speakers, the quality of sound was far *superior*.
- The *lofty* ideals of Gandhiji should be practiced if one wants to evolve as a human being.

Cheat

Syn – Deceive, con, rob, theft, swindle, defraud, fleece, hoodwink, hoax, dupe, delude, trick, beguile, mislead, impostor, rogue, knave.

eg.

- Mothers have an unerring eye about their offspring, and it is not easy to *deceive* them.
- The slick conman managed to *dupe* a number of investors before he was caught.

Ant – Fair, true, aboveboard, just.

eg.

- The employer was *fair* and unbiased in his evaluation report.
- *True* love conquers all.

Check

Syn – Stop, restrain, impede, hinder, control, curb, subdue, repress, match, correspond, mark.

eg.

- The Border Security Force found it difficult to *restrain* the mob.
- The government asked its people to *curb* their expenses in these tough times.

Ant – Speed, hurry, advance, encourage, expedite, accelerate, quicken, hasten, precipitate.

eg.

- Troops *advanced* towards the enemy posts.
- The teacher saw the student *hasten* out of the

lecture hall as soon as she entered.

Cheer

Syn – Comfort, solace, gladden, exhilarate, enliven, applaud, root for, praise, clap.

eg.

- My best friend to *comfort* me when I was distressed.
- The whole school stood up to *root for* the winners.

Ant – Deject, depress, dishearten, sadden, discourage, dampen, decry, deprecate, disparage, vilify, condemn, condole.

eg.

- The sight of the little beggar kid *depressed* me.
- Miriam was *disheartened* by the result of her preboard exams.

Cheerful

Syn – Joyous, blithe, sunny, cheery, jolly, happy, bright, gay, lively.

eg.

- The junior class in my school was a *jolly* lot.
- The flowers bloomed in the little garden, making it look *bright* and *gay.*

Ant – Sullen, gloomy, surly, morose, dour, miserable, downcast, sad, woebegone.

eg.

- Yuvi looked *miserable* when he was denied permission to go out and play.
- The child's parents became sad on hearing that he had tested positive for swine flu.

Chic

Syn – Dashing, fashionable, mod, posh, smart, stylish, swanky, trendy.

eg.

- Maharani Gayatri Devi was both *stylish* and *trendy*.

- My friend recently brought his *swanky* new car for a drive.

Ant – Dowdy, unkempt, drab, dull, dreary.

eg.

- Manan's mother is pretty, but ill-dressed and *dowdy*.
- The beggar had long *unkempt* hair.

Chicanery

Syn – Craftiness, deviousness, slyness, trickery.

eg.

- Shakuni's *craftiness* in the game of dice led to the Pandava's defeat.

- Manohar fired his manager after two customers complained of *trickery* and deceit by him.

Chief

Syn – Premier, main, leading, supreme, principal, cardinal, head, captain, chieftain, ruler, commander, leader.

eg.

- The President is the *commander*-in-chief of the three wings of defence.
- Bombay Dyeing is the *leading* name in Indian suiting and shirting companies.

Ant – Petty, lesser, minor, inferior, subsidiary, subordinate, junior, servant, dependent, parasite, follower, minion.

eg.

- Nakul works as his brother's *subordinate* in the same company.
- Buddha's *followers* requested him to share

his learning with them.

Child

Syn – Baby, infant, toddler, offspring, innocent, childlike, immature.

eg.

- The little boy looked so *innocent* while sleeping.
- Subhadra stopped to play with the *baby* in the pram.

Ant – Adult, mature.

eg.

- All the *adults* of the village got together to elect the 'sarpanch'.
- The resolving of conflicts calls for a *mature* mediator.

Chill

Syn – Coldness, chilliness, cool, freeze, put on ice, shivering, frost, dampen, hostility (used as 'chill in the air')

eg.

- The *cool* mountain breeze soothed my senses.
- The little girl was *shivering* in the cold.

Ant – Warmth, fire, flame, heat, glow, bonfire, fervor.

eg.

- The *fire* in the woods spread quickly.
- The leader's voice had a passionate *fervor*.

Chimera

Syn – Fantasy, illusion, daydream, imagination.

eg.

- Magicians are good at creating *illusion*.
- The student sitting in the last row was caught *daydreaming*.

Ant – Reality.

eg.

- The reporter promised to bring the *reality,* and not fiction, before the readers.

Chip

Syn – Break off, fragment (used as 'chip off the old block'), break, flake, cut, whittle, hew, damage.

eg.

- These plates *chip* very easily.
- The family decided to *break* all ties with the prodigal son.

Choice

Syn – Selection, option, alternative, preference, pick, variety, abundance.

eg.

- The *selection* of candidates depends on their academic grades.
- The students have the *option* of choosing subjects in class XI.

Ant – Refusal, denial, rejection, cancellation.

eg.

- Ajay's *refusal* to part with the money cost him his life.
- The defendant's *denial* of facts angered the judge.

Choke

Syn – Strangle, suffocate, smother, stifle, clog, block, obstruct, throttle.

eg.

- Fat *clogs* the arteries of our heart.
- The criminal tried to *strangle* the witness to death.

Ant – Oxygenate, freshen, ventilate, air.

eg.

- The women retired to the powder room to *freshen* up.
- Chad opened the windows to *ventilate* the room.

Choose

Syn – Select, decide, want, wish, prefer, pick, elect, cull.

eg.

- Raman *wants* to be a pilot.
- The panel had to *select* the best candidate for the post.

Ant – Reject, discard, renounce, spurn, disapprove.

eg.

- The young prince *renounced* the throne and went to the forest.
- The student *discarded* his old books.

Chronic

Syn – Habitual, routine, continuing, prolonged, protracted, lingering, persistent.

eg.

- Charu passed away after a *prolonged* illness.
- The scent of lilies *lingered* on in the air.

Ant – Temporary, passing, fleeting.

eg.

- Farida got a *temporary* posting after her internship.
- Hari saw a *fleeting* glimpse of the girl behind the burqa.

Circulate

Syn – Propagate, flow, go, move, travel, disperse, scatter, strew, spread, advertise, mix, socialize, publish.

eg.

- Priya loves to meet friends and *socialize* in her free time.
- The exhaust fan ensures constant *flow* of fresh air.

Ant – Restrict, repress.

eg.

- The library rules *restrict* the usage of certain reference books.
- Freud ascribes most psychological disorders to *repressed* desires.

Circumscribe

Syn – Bound, contain, encircle, enclose, envelope, surround, encompass.

eg.

- The car *encircled* the house twice before entering it.

- The mist *enveloped* the valley.

Claim

Syn – Maintain, assert, say, state, require, declare, argue, assume, challenge, demand.

eg.

- The boy *asserted* his right to call a lawyer.
- The Principal *demanded* an explanation.

Ant – Waive, drop, forgo, yield, renounce.

eg.

- The government decided to *waive* off the taxes for the current year.
- The victim's family agreed to *drop* the charges against the accused.

Class

Syn – Group, set, rank, division, rank, distribute, classify, arrange.

eg.

- We *classify* the plant kingdom into smaller groups based on their common characteristics.
- The students were asked to *arrange* the numbers in ascending order.

Ant – Disarrange, display, upset, disorder, confuse, derange.

eg.

- The movers and packers company *disarranged* the furniture in order to dismantle it.
- There was *disorder* and *confusion* in the apartment which had been ransacked.

Clean

Syn – Purify, spotless, dirt-free, unsoiled, hygienic, fresh, sanitary, sparkling.

eg.

- The housekeeper sorted the *unsoiled* laundry, and put the rest for washing.
- The Kumar's mansion was *spotlessly* clean at all times.

Ant – Corrupt, dirty, infect, defile, soil, pollute, taint.

eg.

- A *dirty* kitchen leads straight to the doctor.

- Ria *soiled* her clothes while playing in the garden.

Clear

Syn – Definite, free, pay off, solve, clarify (used as 'clear doubts') acquit, exonerate, visible, obvious, distinct, apparent, plain, lucid, unmistakable, explicit.

eg.

- It was *apparent* from the teacher's expression that Neil had done well.
- The ring of Saturn was *distinct* and *unmistakable.*

Ant – Blurred, confused, doubtful, foggy, vague, unintelligible.

eg.

- Puri was disturbed about his *blurred* vision.
- Manan was *confused* about which subjects to take in class XI.

Clever

Syn – Talented, bright, intelligent, gifted, capable, smart, dexterous, natural, quick, witty, brainy, sharp.

eg.

- Ali's teacher thinks that he is a *gifted* child.
- The Shaw sisters are so *talented* that their school decided to give them a scholarship.

Ant – Foolish, dull, doltish, incapable, stupid.

eg.

- All work and no play make Jack a *dull* boy.
- The professors thought that Roshan was a *stupid* boy.

Cling

Syn – Attach, grip, adhere, stick, cleave, clutch, embrace, hold, hug.

eg.

- The Buddhist monks have to *adhere* to the principles of Buddhism.

- Little Anna *gripped* her mother's hand tightly.

Ant – Surrender, give up forgo, relinquish, resign, cede.

eg.

- Kanav made up his mind to *give up* smoking.
- The defeated king had to *surrender* before the victor.

Cloudy

Syn – Gloomy, dark, dim, gray, murky, foggy, overcast.

eg.

- The *overcast* skies promised a day of thunder and showers.
- The woods looked mysterious on the *foggy* morning.

Ant – Sunny, undimmed, unclouded, clear, bright.

eg.

- The day of the picnic dawned *bright* and *sunny.*
- The poor old man's eyes were *undimmed* despite years of struggle.

Clutch

Syn – Grip, hold, seize, catch, grab, grasp.

eg.

- A man's reach should not exceed his *grasp.*
- Little children ran around in the garden trying to *catch* butterflies.

Ant – Release, liberate, emancipate.

eg.

- Freedom fighters fought to *liberate* our country.
- The prisoner was *released* after he completed his sentence.

Coarse

Syn – Unpolished, harsh, unrefined, rude, gross, indelicate.

eg.

- The shopkeeper pointed out the pile of *unrefined* pulses in the corner.

- Binati shielded her eyes against the *harsh* sunlight.

Ant – Polished, polite, elegant, refined, civilized, genteel.

eg.

- The dietician explained the drawbacks of having *refined* flour to the patient.
- Finishing schools promise to *polish* young girls into sophisticated women.

Combat

Syn – War, battle, struggle, action, contest, conflict, broil.

eg.

- The soldier who lost his life in *action* was awarded posthumously.
- The actor had to *struggle* for a long time before he got a decent break.

Ant – Harmony, peace, concord, amity, agreement, quiet.

eg.

- The two warring nations promised to live in *harmony*.
- The companies signed the *agreement* to merge.

Comfort

Syn – Soothe, console, reassure, ease, rest, leisure, relaxation, repose, relief.

eg.

- A good holiday should include time for *relaxation* as well as sightseeing.
- We tried to *console* our grieving friend.

Ant – Unrest, restlessness, agitation, nervousness.

eg.

- There was *unrest* in the city after police firing.
- There was *agitation* in the students when the wrong question paper was given.

Comfortable

Syn – At ease, contented, relaxing, pleasing, convenient, pleasant.

eg.

- The old woman was *at ease* in her house.

- The small boy looked quite *contented* with his new toy.

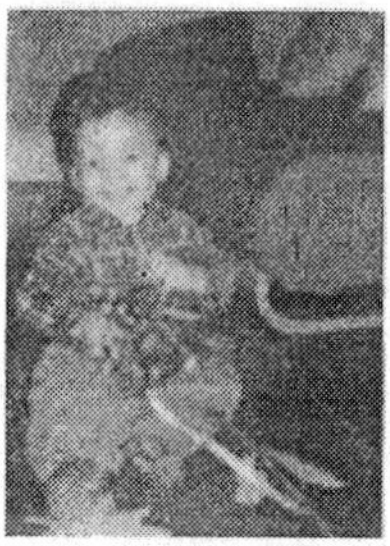

Ant – Irritating, disagreeable, displeasing, aggravating, distressed, disturbed.

eg.

- My sister is very *irritating*.
- Harshal's mother was *distressed* to hear that he had been rusticated from school.

Command

Syn – Domination, authority, control, order, directive, mandate, rule, behest, decree, direct.

eg.

- The island was under the direct *control* of the Queen.
- The state government had to comply with the *directive* issued by the central government.

Ant – Comply, submit, obey.

eg.

- The students were asked to *submit* their assignments on time.
- We must *obey* our elders.

Common

Syn – Usual, widespread, frequent, general, ordinary, familiar, vulgar, mean, trite, hackneyed, low.

eg.

- It felt nice to be back in the *familiar* place.
- The swine flu became a *widespread* epidemic in no time at all.

Ant – Unusual, infrequent, extraordinary, exceptional, unfamiliar, refined, cultured, polished, genteel.

eg.

- It is always nice to mix with a *cultured* crowd.
- The *genteel* woman smiled at the beggar before giving him alms.

Companion

Syn – Friend, colleague, pal, buddy, shadow, accomplice, associate, comrade.

eg.

- Jerry's *friend* took him out for coffee.
- Nihal's *accomplice* confessed before the police.

Ant – Enemy, rival, partisan, unsportsmanlike.

eg.

- The *rival* team gave a standing ovation to the winner.
- The best way to conquer an *enemy* is to make him your friend.

Company

Syn – Troupe, collection, crowd, assemblage, group, gathering, firm, assembly, gang, house, corporation, band.

eg.

- The *crowd* gave a thunderous applause after the speech.
- The *gang* split up after the leader died.

Ant – Individual, isolated, alone, single.

eg.

- Each *individual* can contribute to the well being of the society.
- No man needs to be *alone* until he chooses to be.

Comparison

Syn – Contrast, judgment, assessment, association.

eg.

- The *contrast* between the two sibling's personalities was too stark.
- The colonel's *assessment* of the situation turned out to be fairly accurate.

Compassion

Syn – Kindness, tenderness, empathy, concern, mercy, sympathy, condolence.

eg.

- Her *concern* for her brother's well being was obvious.
- A doctor can cure his patients better if he combines *tenderness* with good medicines.

Ant – Cruelty, brutality, savagery.

eg.

- The little boy was infamous for his *cruelty* towards animals.
- The *savagery* faced by the Jews under Hitler's regime made headlines.

Compel

Syn – Bind, coerce, drive, oblige, force, twist one's arm, constrain, necessitate.

eg.

- The school bully *forced* Garun to act like a monkey.
- Chandru's friends *coerced* him to bunk classes and go for a movie.

Ant – Acquit, induce, allure, invite, tempt.

eg.

- Shreya's friends *invited* her to join the doll's birthday party.
- Isha was *tempted* to skip work on her birthday.

Compose

Syn – Write, pacify, form, compile, arrange, create, calm.

eg.

- Teacher asked the class to *write* an original story.
- The young bride took deep breaths to *calm* herself.

Ant – Excite, irritate, criticize, dissect.

eg.

- The media tries to *excite* and sensationalize, rather than solve.
- The little boy could see that his mother was getting *irritated.*

Compress

Syn – Abridge, squeeze, squash, reduce, constrict, contract, compact, condense.

eg.

- Suri *squashed* the mosquito with her racquet.

- All the family members *squeezed* in the little car.

Ant – Diffuse, dilate, expand.

eg.

- Her eyes *dilate*d with fear.
- The balloon *expanded* with air.

Conceal

Syn – Suppress, cover up, obscure, screen, mask, disguise, hide.

eg.

- The political leader tried to *cover up* the murder of the journalist.
- The stars try to *hide* behind large sunglasses.

Ant – Expose, confess, reveal, manifest.

eg.

- The sting operation *exposed* the corrupt official.
- The reporter tried to *reveal* the truth about the minister.

Concord

Syn – Unity, peace, friendship, harmony, amity, accord.

eg.

- The government urged the citizens to maintain *peace* and order.
- It is important for neighbors to live in *harmony*.

Ant – Animosity, variance, discord, disagreement.

eg.

- There was open *animosity* between the two warring tribes.
- The views of the opposition leader were at *variance* with the ruling party.

Concrete

Syn – Consolidated, real, tangible, existing, actual, solid, compact, firm.

eg.

- The police did not have any *tangible* proof of Munna's involvement in the crime.

- The threat of global warming is both *real* and frightening.

Ant – Loose, shifting, sloppy.

eg.

- The *shifting* sands of time bring change in man's life.
- Turani did a *sloppy* job with the project in hand.

Confess

Syn – Acknowledge, admit, reveal, come clean, own, aver.

eg.

- Manju *admitted* her mistake to the teacher.
- The petty thief promised to *come clean* before the magistrate.

Ant – Deny, suppress, disavow.

eg.

- The accused *denied* the allegations.
- The commissioner tried his best to *suppress* the facts of the case.

Confine

Syn – Bind, narrow, imprison, detain, bound, impound, incarcerate, limit.

eg.

- The lion was *bound* in chains inside his cage.

- The judge asked the police to *imprison* the terrorist at once.

Ant – Extend, expand, loosen, widen, release.

eg.

- The central government announced the *release* of 200 prisoners on Republic Day.
- The last date for filling application forms was *extended* by the commission.

Confirm

Syn – Fix, prove, strengthen, corroborate, verify, substantiate, authenticate.

eg.

- The detective was asked to *verify* that the claimant had not committed a fraud

- Pranab added statistics to *substantiate* his viewpoint in the report.

Ant – Cancel, upset, refute, repeal, shake.

eg.

- The director *cancelled* the exam after the question paper leaked.
- The TV channel *refuted* the claims made by the advertisement.

Conquest

Syn – Overthrow, occupation, invasion, victory, triumph.

eg.

- The king's *triumph* over the enemy was celebrated by his subjects.
- Our freedom fighters made plans to *overthrow* the British rule.

Ant – Forfeiture, surrender, retreat, defeat.

eg.

- The criminal decided to *surrender* to the police.
- The students felt sad after the school team's *defeat* in basketball.

Conscientious

Syn – Uncorrupt, principled, careful, thorough, meticulous, faithful, diligent, assiduous, honorable.

eg.

- Manohar is a *diligent* boy.
- Rani is *meticulous* with planning finer details.

Ant – Corrupt, profligate, wicked, vile.

eg.

- The *corrupt* officer was fired by his superior.
- The *wicked* boy killed the little pup.

Constant

Syn – Steady, firm, stable, unswerving, invariable, unvarying, steadfast.

eg.

- Tulsidas was *unswerving* in his devotion for Lord Rama.

- Slow and *steady* wins the race.

Ant – Unsteady, flexible, variable, inconsonant, unreliable, unstable, fickle.

eg.

- Fortune, that *fickle* lady of uncertain virtue!
- Most network operators offer *flexible* talk time plans.

Contemptible

Syn – Despicable, vile, shameful, disgraceful, detestable, loathsome.

eg.

- The *disgraceful* incident at school left her embittered for life.
- Shawn tried to put the *shameful* episode behind him.

Ant – Respectable, admirable, noble, excellent, weighty, grave, important.

eg.

- The freedom fighters fought for a *noble* cause.
- The middle-aged couple looked quite *respectable*.

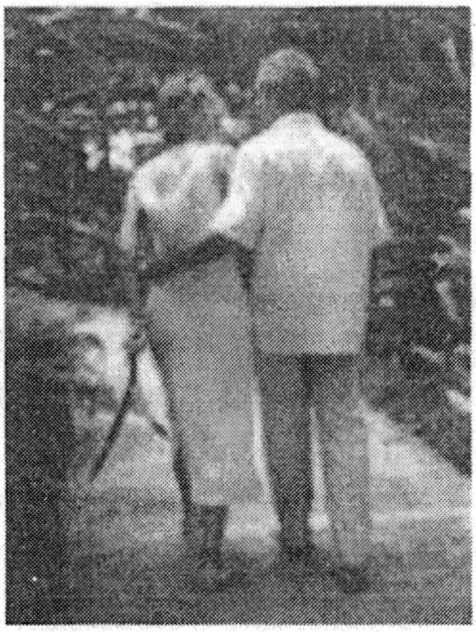

Convict

Syn – Condemn, sentence, criminal, offender, crook, villain, prisoner.

eg.

- Damian is a small time *crook*.
- The judge awarded the unrepentant criminal the maximum *sentence*.

Ant – Discharge, acquit.

eg.

- The medical superintendent decided to *discharge* the patient.
- The accused was *acquitted* by the judge.

Corrupt

Syn – Dishonest, shady, fraudulent, crooked, pollute,

impair, spoil, infect, putrefy, defile, decay.

eg.

- The honest officer decided to stay out of the *fraudulent* deal.
- The virus in the PC *infected* my hard drive.

Ant – Cleanse, purify, repair, mend, pure, undefiled, uninfected.

eg.

- Chanting and meditation *cleanse* the soul.
- The electrician came to *mend* my water cooler.

D

Dabb

Syn – Daub, apply, wipe, pat, blob, touch lightly.

eg.

- Melanie *wiped* her tears with a handkerchief.
- She *dabbed* some cream on her face.

Dabble

Syn – Experiment, try your hand at, dip into, play at.

eg.

- Sabhyata wants to *experiment* with meditation as a means of relaxation.

- Her children wanted to *dabble* in painting in their free time.

Daft

Syn – Silly, stupid, foolish, dippy, dense, thick, dim-witted.

eg.

- He behaved like a *dim-witted* puppy when his girlfriend was around.
- "Don't be *daft,*" chided his sister when she saw him looking so lovesick.

Ant - Intelligent, clever, bright, smart, sharp.

eg.

- Rea is a sensible and *intelligent* girl.
- Theresa's younger brother seemed quite *sharp.*

Dagger

Syn – Blade, carving knife, switchblade, penknife.

eg.

- The victim had been killed with a *carving knife*.
- The mobster's *blade* glistened in the sun.

Daily

Syn – Everyday, each day.

eg.

- Her father owns the national *daily* newspaper.
- One should take *each day* as it comes.

Ant - Sometime, for a while, once in a while, occasionally.

eg.

- Abodh goes to visit his grandmother *once in a while*.
- Madhavi likes to fast *occasionally*.

Dainty

Syn – Delicate, elegant, graceful, petite, pretty

eg.

- Melinda is a *pretty* girl with *dainty* features.
- That *petite* girl is Vani's sister.

Ant - Coarse, huge, giant, mammoth, ungainly.

eg.

- The *mammoth* building was quite an eyesore.
- The maid had *coarse* and rough hands.

Damage

Syn – Injure, spoil, hurt, harm, break, dent, scratch.

eg.

- The death of a parent can cause serious psychological *damage*.
- Manohar was *hurt* in a climbing accident.

Ant - Repair, mend, fix, restore.

eg.

- Father agreed to *fix* my skateboard in a day or two.

* The artist promised to *restore* old paintings.

Danger

Syn – Risk, peril hazard, menace, threat, jeopardy.

eg.

- Anti social elements are a *menace* to society.
- Plastic poses grave environmental *hazard*.

Ant – Protection, safeguard, defense, safety, security.

eg.

- We have to learn to *safeguard* our own interests.
- The *security* within our country rests on the shoulders of vigilant citizens

Deadly

Syn – Fatal, lethal, mortal, toxic, poisonous, noxious.

eg.

- The vet gave a *lethal* injection to the rabid dog.
- The police deduced that the victim had died after consuming a *poisonous* substance.

Ant – Vital, healthful, life-giving, nutritious.

eg.

- We must include all the *vital* nutrients in our diet.
- Healthy and *nutritious* food makes us strong.

Dear

Syn – Beloved, cherished, expensive, valued, precious, darling, sweetheart.

eg.

- Education was something my mother held very *dear*.
- Mark is a *cherished* friend.

Ant - Cheap, inexpensive.

eg.

- Julie was wearing a *cheap* watch.
- The goods were comparatively *inexpensive* at the wholesale outlet.

Decay

Syn – Deterioration, decompose, rot, molder, fester, sinking, decline, wearing, degeneracy.

eg.

- The police found the *decomposed* body of a woman in the woods.
- Osteoporosis occurs due to *degeneracy* of bones.

Ant – Improvement, progress, expansion, development.

eg.

- Our country has made tremendous *progress* in the last 25 years.
- The blue chip companies assure both *expansion* and growth.

Deceive

Syn – Betray, mislead, dupe, entrap, swindle, con, cheat, trick.

eg.

- Yuri *swindled* the poor old lady.
- The little boy was fascinated by the magician's *trick*.

Ant – Enlighten, guide, advise.

eg.

- A good friend is also a good *guide*.
- Guru Nanak *enlightens* his disciples about religion.

Decent

Syn – Polite, civilized, honest, appropriate, well mannered, upright, straight.

Eg.

- The widow was *appropriately* dressed in black.
- "Don't you have any decent clothes," asked mother in exasperation.

Ant - Indecent, offensive, crude, filthy, impolite, lewd.

Eg.

- Kathy wore an *indecent* dress to the office.
- The boy made a *lewd* gesture with his hands.

Decide

Syn – Settle, fix, determine, choose, resolve.

eg.

- We *choose* our own destiny.
- Siddhant *resolved* not to meet his girlfriend while his exams were going on.

Ant – Hesitate, prevaricate, doubt, fluctuate, waver, waive.

eg.

- Gautam Buddha never *wavered* from the path of righteousness.
- The share prices *fluctuate* very often.

Declare

Syn – Announce, broadcast, assert, proclaim, publish, advertise, enunciate.

eg.

- Abhishek *announced* his plans for the mountaineering trip to his friends.
- "I am not going home till this work gets done," he *asserted.*

Ant – Conceal, censor, withhold, deny.

eg.

- The star *denied* her affair with her driver.
- The judge asked the witness not to *withhold* any information.

Decline

Syn – Reject, refuse, discard, turn down, renounce, sink, degenerate, decrease, lessen, diminish, fall, drop.

eg.

- Shram *discarded his old shirt.*
- Gold prices *dropped* for the first time in a decade.

Ant – Accept, accede to, agree to, admit, grow, aggravate, augment, enhance, increase.

eg.

- Brij *agreed* to escort his sister to the party.
- The accused *admitted* his mistake.

Decode

Syn – Decipher, translate, interpret, crack, work out.

eg.

- This software is used to *decode* the information embedded in the satellite broadcasts.

- An interpreter was summoned to *translate* the minister's speech from Swahili to English.

Ant - Encode, program, instruct, code.

eg.

- The software analyst was called by the Home Ministry to *encode* the confidential data.
- The *program* used by the computer engineer was outdated.

Decorate

Syn – Beautify, adorn, embellish, trim, garnish, bedeck.

eg.

- My drawing room is *decorated* in blue and grey.
- Meira wore an old fashioned dress *embellished* with big buttons and satin ribbons.

Decrease

Syn – Reduce, cut, diminish, lessen, decline, dwindle, shrink.

eg.

- Asthma attacks *reduced* in Grace's early adult life.
- Awareness about global warming has led to a gradual *decrease* in power wastage.

Ant - Increase, augment, amplify, boost, swell, enhance.

eg.

- The political tensions between the two countries have *increased* the chances of war.
- Shares of blue chip companies *enhance* the portfolio of an investor.

Deed

Syn – Action, feat, act, endeavor, exploit, work, accomplishment, achievement, legal deed.

eg.

- The young girl was awarded for her unusual *feat* of courage.

- Children should be encouraged to do random *acts* of kindness.

Deep

Syn – Profound, yawning, cavernous.

eg.

- The castle is on an island surrounded by *deep* waters.
- Hema's views on religion and spirituality have always been rather *profound*.

Ant - Shallow, low, thin, trivial, petty.

eg.

- The lake was *shallow*, but mother still asked us to keep away.
- The *petty* squabbles between the friends led to major showdown.

Defeat

Syn – Overcome, beat, overpower, rout, outwit, conquer, crush, frustrate, fail.

eg.

- The chess champion *beat* his opponent.
- We must learn to *conquer* our fears.

Ant – Prevail, triumph, win, overthrow, vanquish.

eg.

- *Truth* must prevail.
- Our team can *win* the national trophy.

Definite

Syn – Exact, certain, specific, distinct, fixed, explicit, unconditional, unqualified, categorical, unequivocal.

eg.

- The traveler wanted to know the *exact* time.
- My teacher gave *explicit* directions.

Ant – Indefinite, unspecified, unspecific, vague, obscure, tentative, ambiguous, implicit, uncertain, conditional.

eg.

- The signpost was quite *ambiguous.*
- The boy was *vague* about his plans.

Delay

Syn – Hold, keep, wait, detain, setback, impediment, retard.

eg.

- The doctor's secretary asked me to *wait* in the clinic.

- Paul was *detained* by the director after office hours.

Ant – Quicken, speed, hasten, further.

eg.

- The strong medicine *hastened* his recovery.
- Sam tried to *further* his prospects by accepting a better job offer.

Delicacy

Syn – Smoothness, softness, frailty, fragility, elegance, refinement, slenderness, lightness.

eg.

- The star was admired for her *elegance.*
- Evening gowns suited her *slender* frame.

Ant – Roughness, hardness, sturdiness, robustness, crudeness, heaviness.

eg.

- The geologists studied the rocks by examining their *hardness.*
- The little sapling grew into a *sturdy* tree.

Deliver

Syn – Bring, transport, carry, distribute, send, convey, hand over.

eg.

- The ship *carried* the cargo to its destination.
- The messenger *conveyed* the message to the king.

Ant – Arrest, imprison, catch, seize, keep.

eg.

- The policeman *arrested* the thief.
- Kapil missed the last *catch* of the over.

Describe

Syn – Explain, relate, illustrate, portray, depict, define, narrate, recount, tell.

eg.

- Huma *narrated* the incident to her mother.
- The teacher *explained* the theory of relativity to the student.

Ant – Falsify, mystify, misrepresent, suppress.

eg.

- He was arrested because he tried to *falsify* accounts.
- The witness tried to *suppress* facts.

Description

Syn – Account, explanation, report, portrayal, picture, narrative, sketch, depiction.

eg.

- The author's *portrayal* of the slums was very realistic.
- Jehann's mother listened to his *account* of the incident.

Despair

Syn – Despondency, misery, anguish, dejection, gloom, desperation, hopelessness, discouragement.

eg.

- The *misery* on the old woman's face made me feel sad too.
- There was a pall of *gloom* when the school team lost the match.

Ant – Confidence encouragement, elation, hope, optimism.

eg.

- The coach cheered his team with words of *encouragement*.
- The new president ushered in a new era of *hope* and *optimism*.

Despise

Syn – Hate, abhor, deride, scorn, spurn, loathe, disdain.

eg.

- The little girl *hated* her wicked stepmother.
- I *loathe* liars.

Ant – Admire, adore, like, love, respect, appreciate.

eg.

- Devika *adores* her little brother.
- Antara *appreciated* her sister's attempt to help her.

Destroy

Syn – Ruin, raze, obliterate, uproot, wreck, waste, demolish, annihilate, eradicate, exterminate, extinguish.

eg.

- Archaeologists study the *ruins* to understand the life and times of people living in those times.
- The noble police officer tried to *exterminate* anti-social elements.

Ant – Make, repair, restore, reinstate, build, create, devise, establish.

eg.

- M F Hussain has *created* many beautiful masterpieces.

- Payal *restores* old paintings.

Detail

Syn – Feature, point, element, aspect, fact, factor.

eg.

- Rajesh had planned the journey down to the smallest *detail.*
- This *aspect* of the process will be more thoroughly discussed in chapter 8.

Detect

Syn – Notice, sense, perceive, spot, distinguish, identify.

eg.

- Isha *detected* a note of sarcasm in her friend's voice.
- An enemy aircraft was *identified* on the radar.

Ant - Latent, dormant, covert.

eg.

- The volcano erupted after lying *dormant* for the last five years or so.

- A *covert* operation to catch the terrorist was underway.

Determination

Syn – Willpower, resolve, fortitude, purpose, grit, strength of mind.

eg.

- Mishra shows great *determination* to learn his work and better his prospects.
- Shraddha has the *willpower* to lose weight.

Ant - Weakness.

eg.

- She has a *weakness* for ice creams.

Development

Syn – Growth, improvement, expansion, progress, adv-ance, increase, maturity, events.

eg.

- My course in English Major has a paper on the *development* of the Greek thought.
- The news channels keep us updated about the latest *events.*

Deviate

Syn – Diverge, swerve, str-ay, depart, wander, digress, vary, differ.

eg.

- The official became restless when the eld-erly gentleman *digressed* yet again from the point
- Our paths *diverged* when our jobs took us to diffe-rent cities.

Ant – Converge, stay, perpe-tuate, continue, pervade, abide.

eg.

- My mother always insisted that I *stay* on the right side of the law.
- Students are expected to *abide* by the school rules.

Differ

Syn – Vary, fluctuate, change, diverge, disagree.

eg.

- My brother and I *differ* in our ability to handle stress.
- The market index *fluctuates* regularly.

Different

Syn – Diverse, unlike, dissimilar, unusual, special, singular.

eg.

- The study proved that women had significantly *different* eating patterns from men.
- The *diverse* cultures of his adopted country enriched his personality.

Ant - Same, similar, alike, equal, equivalent.

eg.

- The friends shared *similar* political views.
- The twins looked, dressed and behaved *alike.*

Difficult

Syn – Complicated, complex, hard, tricky, intricate.

eg.

- The mathematics professor gave us a *complicated* problem to solve.
- Harsh is finding it *difficult* to get a job.

Ant - Easy, simple, effortless, uncomplicated.

eg.

- The Sharmas found that it was *easy* to replace rather than repair electrical gadgets.

- The ballet dancer made the dance look *effortless* and graceful.

Diligent

Syn – Careful, hardworking, assiduous, industrious, meticulous, laborious, attentive, busy, painstaking.

eg.

- Soha is very *attentive* in class.
- The little girl is very *meticulous* with her projects.

Ant – Slack, lazy, indolent, idle, slothful.

eg.

- Shweta loves to sit *idle* and gossip.
- Ashwin became *slack* in his work after his illness.

Disappoint

Syn – Defeat, vex, baffle, foil, thwart, frustrate, disillusion, deceive.

eg.

- The student was *baffled* by the professor's question.
- The girl *foiled* the robber's attempt.

Ant – Satisfy, gratify, fulfill, justify.

eg.

- The dog felt *satisfied* after chasing the vendor out of the lane.
- The ends do not *justify* the means.

Disgrace

Syn – Degrade, humiliate, ignominy, shame, disparage, discredit, dishonor.

eg.

- The girl was blamed for bringing *shame* to the family name.
- Those advertisements which are *degrading* to women should be banned.

Ant – Honor, reverence, respect, exalt, dignify, elevate, venerate.

eg.

- The subjects showed *reverence* to their dictator.
- We must *respect* our elders.

Distant

Syn – Far-away, far-flung, isolated, inaccessible, remote, asunder.

eg.

- The traders had to go to *far-away* lands for trade and commerce.
- The reporter went to *remote* tribal areas to make a documentary.

Ant – Accessible, close, proximate, contiguous, adjacent.

eg.

- The market is quite *close* to our house.
- The two friends bought *adjacent* houses.

Domestic

Syn – Home, family, household, marital, conjugal.

eg.

- Unfortunately, Hiten's *marital* life was not very happy.
- Nowadays couples are more willing to share *domestic* chores.

Ant - International, global, worldwide.

eg.

- The growing technology has linked us to each other and made the whole world a *global* village.
- There is a *worldwide* growing concern for curbing terrorism.

Dominate

Syn – Control, rule, lead, govern, direct, dictate.

eg.

- Saira's loud voice *dominated* the conversation.
- The rising prices *dictate* the consumers' choice of household products.

Ant - Follow, comply, obey.

eg.

- She decided to *follow* her sister's advice.
- She wanted to *comply* with her family's wishes.

Doubt

Syn – Suspicion, hesitation, skepticism, uncertainty, distrust, disbelief, qualm.

eg.

- There was *distrust* between the family members.
- There was *disbelief* on the kid's face when the magician pulled out a rabbit from his hat.

Ant – Certainty, confidence, conviction, assurance.

eg.

- The leader gave *assurance* that the killers would be caught.
- She replied with *certainty* that her master did not do it.

Dreadful

Syn – Frightful, dire, terrible, alarming, awful, horrible.

eg.

- The *frightful* man scared the children.
- Rattan was in *dire* need of money.

Ant – Pleasing, pleasurable, propitious, reassuring, auspicious.

eg.

- Heera's parents waited for an *auspicious* day to fix her marriage.
- The boys waited for a *propitious* moment to break the news.

Dry

Syn – Parched, arid, barren, tedious, dehydrated, crisp, desiccated.

eg.

- Shubhra needed a *desiccated* coconut to prepare the dish.
- The *arid* desert looked dry and *barren*.

Ant – Damp, wet, moistened, fresh, lively, moist, soggy.

eg.

- Vibha served the *fresh* cake straight out of the oven.

- The earth was *damp* after the showers.

E

Each

Syn – Every, all, both, every one.

eg.

- She had a bottle in *each* hand.
- "Every speaker gets three minutes to make their presentation."

Ant - None, nobody.

eg.

- There was *nobody* home.
- There is *none* so blind as one who has eyes and won't see.

Eager

Syn – Desirous, keen, raring to go, enthusiastic, excited, fervent, impatient, zealous.

eg.

- Sara was very *enthusiastic* about painting.
- The *zealous* followers set fire to the effigies.

Ant – Unconcerned, indifferent, apathetic, loath, disinterested.

eg.

- Shreyas was *indifferent* to the plight of the laborers.
- The management was *apathetic* towards the employees.

Ear

Syn – Hearing, grain (used as 'ear of corn').

eg.

- I don't know why I tell her anything; it just goes in one *ear* and out from the other.
- She came out of the interview room beaming from *ear* to *ear*.

Early

Syn – Near the beginning, early on, untimely, premature, before time.

eg.

- She went out *early* in the morning.
- The young soldier met with an *untimely* demise.

Ant - Late, behind, delayed, overdue.

eg.

- Thenny lagged *behind* in the race.

- The trains were *delayed* because of a storm.

Earn

Syn – Gain, win, get, bring in, make, receive, achieve, acquire, merit.

eg.

- Ira was happy to *win* the title.
- God says, "Ask, and you shall *receive*."

Ant – Waste, spend, forgo, forfeit, lose.

eg.

- We should not *waste* our resources.
- Paheli did not want to *lose* her friend.

Easy

Syn – Simple, effortless, pain-less, uncomplicated, comfor-table, relaxed, friendly.

eg.

- Tourists are an *easy* prey for thieves.
- The guests enjoyed the *friendly* and *relaxed* atmosphere at Raphael's house.

Ant - Difficult, hard, tricky, complicated, complex, intricate.

eg.

- The new recruits found the exercise regimen very *difficult* to follow.
- The new software was very *complicated* to use.

Ebb

Syn – Wane, decline, go out, flow away, retire, sink, recede.

eg.

- The tide *receded* by late noon.
- The waxing and *waning* of the moon affects the tide.

Ant – Flow, increase, abound, swell.

eg.

- The company's cash *flow* was affected by recession.
- The *swelling* on mother's face *increased* in the evening.

Eccentric

Synonyms - Odd, unconven-tional, peculiar, strange, weird.

eg.

- I found my *eccentric* old uncle amusing rather than irritating.

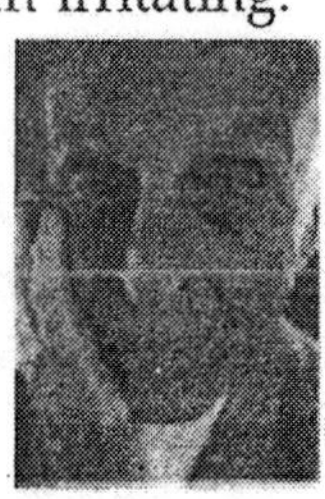

- The accused had a *peculiar* look in the eyes.

Ant - Normal, usual, ordinary, typical.

eg.

- The girl looked and talked like a *typical* teenager.
- The school canteen chef served the *usual* insipid fare with a smile.

Elegant

Syn – Stylish, graceful, chic, luxurious, grandiose, sumptuous, deluxe.

eg.

- The sophisticated woman looked *chic* in the designer gown.

- Mona is very *stylish* and always very immaculately turned out.

Ant – Inexpensive, plain, mediocre, unadorned, simple, usual, vulgar.

eg.

- My teacher did not want the project to look *plain* and *simple*.

- Reshma's dress was tacky and *vulgar*.

Eliminate

Syn – Eradicate, remove, abolish, reduce.

eg.

- The doctor advised us to *eliminate* fatty food from our diet.
- Slavery is an evil, and should be *abolished*.

Ant - Include, comprise, incorporate.

eg.

- The architect has *incorporated* environment friendly features into the design of this building.
- The athlete's diet *includes* protein, carbohydrates and all the vital nutrients in a balanced proportion.

Enchanted

Syn – Charmed, fascinated, bewitched, enthralled, captivated, enraptured, enamored, entranced, spellbound.

eg.

- The prince was *enamored* by the beautiful and mysterious Cinderella.
- Krishna's flute notes held the villagers *spellbound*.

Ant – Disgusted, repulsed, repelled, nauseated.

eg.

- Sheila felt *repulsed* by the ugly doorman.
- Rambha was *disgusted* by her brother's behavior.

Encourage

Syn – Back up, animate, urge, incite, cheer, embolden, foster, hearten, support, promote.

eg.

- Tanya *urged* her brother to study harder.
- The party promised to *support* the candidate.

Ant – Dissuade, discourage, dishearten, thwart, hinder.

eg.

- The coach tried to *dissuade* the player from becoming aggressive.
- My teacher *discouraged* me from appearing for the exam.

Encroach

Syn – Infringe, violate, impinge, invade, intrude, trespass.

eg.

- The teenager thought that his parents *invaded* his privacy.
- The article *infringed* the copyright law.

Ant – Withdraw.

eg.

- The commander decided to *withdraw* the army.

Endless

Syn – Unceasing, boundless, continual, incessant, eternal, everlasting, infinite.

eg.

- There was *incessant* chatter in the classroom.
- Hindu philosophy believes in the *eternal* nature of the soul.

Ant – Temporary, brief, fugitive, limited.

eg.

- My friend told me the story in *brief.*
- The camp had *limited* ration.

Enlarge

Syn – Augment, expand, amplify, broaden, widen, magnify, extend, add to, increase.

eg.

- Sulabh *magnified* his own problems.
- Good speakers *amplify* the sound.

Ant – Contact, condense, narrow, shorten, reduce, decrease.

eg.

- The *narrow* lane ended in a cul-de-sac.
- A ban on honking *reduces* noise pollution.

Enmity

Syn – Hostility, hate, discord, antagonism, rancor, animosity.

eg.

- The marital *discord* between the couple made the children unhappy.
- The differences between the brothers soon led to open *animosity.*

Ant – Amity, love, harmony, fellowship, sympathy.

eg.

- The little puppy craved *love* and *sympathy.*

- The two neighboring countries lived in *harmony.*

Enough

Syn – Adequate, abundant, ample, plenty, sufficient.

eg.

- Our mango tree was laden with *ample* fruit for the whole family.
- Myra's family has sufficient resources to lead a comfortable life.

Ant – Insufficient, paucity, inadequate, scarcity, deficient.

eg.

- The *scarcity* of rains led to poor agricultural produce this year.
- Maina's bank had *insufficient* funds in this accounting year.

Enrage

Syn – Anger, madden, incense, infuriate.

eg.

- The little boy was *angry* with his teacher.
- The fidgety pup *infuriated* Param.

Ant – Pacify, mollify, soothe, tranquilize, placate.

eg.

- Tarini was *pacified* by her friend's conciliatory tone.
- Mother tried to *placate* my brother when he fought with me.

Entire

Syn – Whole, full, complete, intact, total.

eg.

- He overhauled his *total* wardrobe.
- The executive went in for a *complete* health check-up.

Ant – Broken, partial, incomplete, limited.

eg.

- The servant collected the *broken* pieces of the glass.
- The doctor told Neema's family that she had suffered *partial* paralysis.

Entry

Syn – Admission, entrance, access, way in, door, opening.

eg.

- The police could see no signs of a forced *entry.*
- *Entry* to the concert was restricted to those who had an *admission* pass.

Ant - Exit, door, outlet, egress.

eg.

- Two men were blocking her *exit.*
- We made for the nearest *exit door.*

Envelope

Syn – Cover, wrapping, covering, packet, cloak, shroud.

eg.

- She tore open the *envelope,* knowing fully well the message it carried.
- In the mornings, mist *shrouded* the forest making them look mysterious.

Equal

Syn – Equivalent, identical, as good.

eg.

- She wasn't his *equal* in either intelligence or looks.
- The Korean company proved to be *as good* as its US counterparts.

Ant - Unequal, asymmetrical, disparate, uneven.

eg.

- The instructor had to face the difficulties of dealing with many *disparate* groups of people.
- The *asymmetrical* dress became quite a rage back in the 80s.

Erase

Syn – Remove, wipe, expunge, obliterate.

eg.

- Some of the names in the teacher's diary had been accidentally *erased*.
- Mohan wanted to *expunge* the bad memory of his first date from his mind.

Ant - Imprint, print, mark.

eg.

- He took the *imprint* of her hand on the soft sand.
- Vivekananda left an indelible *mark* on Indian philosophy.

Evasion

Syn – Dodging, avoidance, skirting, subterfuge, excuse, prevarication.

eg.

- The leader was good at *dodging* tricky questions.
- Panna's *excuse* for missing class was very lame.

Evident

Syn – Clear, visible, plain, apparent, obvious, patent, manifest, distinct.

eg.

- The night sky was so *clear* that it seemed studded with millions of twinkling stars.

- It was *apparent* to the teachers that Vipul was lying.

Ant – Hidden, obscure, secret, covert, latent, masked.

eg.

- The three friends shared a *secret* which no one else knew about.
- The five *masked* men entered the bank and looted it.

Excellent

Syn – Superb, outstanding, brilliant, first-class, prime, first-rate.

eg.

- Brinda prepared a *superb* feast for the guests.
- Akhilesh is a *brilliant* mathematician.

Ant – Mediocre, imperfect, faulty, second-class.

eg.

- Chetan is a *mediocre* student.
- The teacher asked Krish to improve the *faulty* model.

Excite

Syn – Stimulate, provoke, enthuse, motivate, inflame, animate.

eg.

- The TV newscaster *provoked* the speaker into saying more than he wanted to.
- Pratibha's friend tried to *motivate* her to join the gym.

Ant – Compose, soothe, allay, hush, mollify, quell, appease, lull.

eg.

- The young girl seemed quite calm and *composed*.
- The journalist *hushed* the scandal by denying the whole report.

Exertion

Syn – Energy, strain, effort, action.

eg.

- It requires a great deal of *energy* to keep up with small children.
- The police officers put in *effort* to control the crowd.

Ant – Rest, repose, peace, tranquility.

eg.

- Tina likes to *rest* in the afternoons.
- The government urged the citizens to maintain *peace* and order.

Extravagant

Syn – Lavish, profligate, wasteful, excessive, immoderate, spendthrift.

eg.

- The Malhotras threw a *lavish* reception for their daughter.
- Kamini is a *spendthrift*.

Ant – Moderate, temperate, economical, thrifty.

eg.

- My sister asked me to be *moderate* in my expenditure.
- Her old uncle is a rich but *thrifty* gentleman.

F

Fable

Syn – Tale, story, legend, allegory, parable, myth.

eg.

- I read out the Aesop's *fable* about the fox and the crow to my class.
- The *legend* of the virtuous Queen Padmini has few parallels in Indian history.

Ant - Fact, reality.

eg.

- I know this for a *fact* that Mark was present for Salim's birthday party.
- When John joined medical school, he realized that the *reality* was very different from his imagination.

Fabric

Syn – Cloth, material, textile, stuff, foundation, frame-work.

eg.

- Jyoti was looking for some colorful cotton *fabric*.
- Drug abuse poses a major threat to the basic *framework* of our society.

Fabulous

Syn – Wonderful, tremendous, splendid, marvelous, remarkable, amazing, extraordinary.

Eg.

- She looked *fabulous* in the new dress.
- The speech of the new minister was *extraordinary*.

Ant - Terrible, awful, appalling, horrifying.

eg.

- The *terrible* tragedy shook the little town out of its complacence.
- The captive narrated a *horrifying* saga of torture.

Face

Syn – Features, mug, visage, façade, expression, look, appearance.

eg.

- Right through my class, my sister was making *faces* at me through the window.

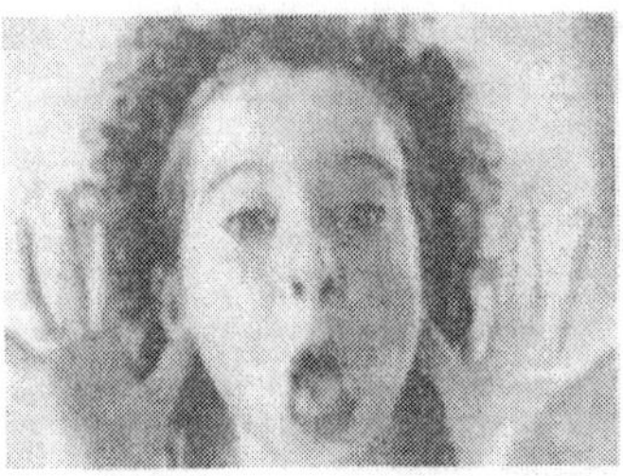

- Her house had an impressive design with a red brick *façade*.

Facility

Syn – Ability, capability, flair, competence.

eg.

- Is there a call-waiting *facility* on this telephone?
- She has an amazing *flair* for languages.

Fact

Syn – Detail, truth, reality, information.

eg.

- Given the *fact* that this was Charan's first match, I think he played quite well.
- The *truth* about Marilyn Monroe's tragic death never reached the public.

Antonyms - Fiction, myth.

eg.

- The star did everything in his power to maintain the *fiction* of his happy childhood.

- Contrary to popular *myth,* most accidents are not caused by drunken driving.

Fame

Syn – Repute, honor, glory, renown, distinction, recognition, prominence, eminence, credit, reputation.

eg.

- A soldier's *glory* lies not in his medals but in the sincere discharge of his duty.
- Karna had the *honor* of being the eldest Pandava.

Ant – Disrepute, dishonor, notoriety, oblivion.

eg.

- The thief's *notoriety* preceded him.
- The aging superstar slowly sank into *oblivion.*

Fanciful

Syn – Imaginary, far-fetched, unreal, whimsical, imaginative, fantastic.

eg.

- The *fantastic* world of fairy tales is brought alive in Disneyland.
- Fortune is a *whimsical* lady, bestowing favors erratically and illogically.

Ant – Realistic, existent, factual, veritable.

eg.

- This movie is a *realistic* portrayal of life in the slums.
- The policeman asked for a *factual* narration of the events following the accident.

Fat

Syn – Stout, overweight, portly, obese, heavy, plump, adipose, chubby, buxom.

eg.

- The *stout* man stamped his foot in anger.
- Sheela has become *plump* now.

Ant – Emaciated, thin, slim.

eg.

- Tulip became *thin* after going to the hostel.
- The old woman looked *emaciated* and undernourished.

Fatal

Syn – Lethal, mortal, deadly, terminal, serious, grave, critical.

eg.

- The killer had given the woman a *lethal* injection.
- She was suffering from a *termina*l disease.

Ant – Life-giving, helpful, beneficial, constructive.

eg.

- The experiment on the new *life-giving* drugs is not yet successful.
- The tuitions were *helpful* in clarifying his concepts.

Feeble

Syn – Weak, impotent, frail, infirm, delicate, shabby, meager.

eg.

- The girl looked quite *frail* in the white muslin dress.

- The *infirm* old gentleman became quite cranky.

Ant – Strong, vigorous, muscular, athletic, stalwart, robust, sinewy.

eg.

- The boy looked *robust* and healthy.
- The *muscular* young boy was an ace basketball player.

Final

Syn – Last, ultimate, concluding, finishing.

eg.

- The writer finished the *concluding* chapter of his book.
- The *last* over of the match was the most interesting.

Ant – First, beginning, opening, initial.

eg.

- The *first* rain of the season was very refreshing.

- After the *initial* struggle, Ambika became very successful.

Find

Syn – Locate, learn, unearth, stumble upon, detect, uncover, ascertain, discover.

eg.

- The archaeologist *unearthed* the hidden treasures.
- The little boy tried to *locate* the remote village on the map.

Ant – Forget, mislay, miss.

eg.

- Sara *forgot* to take the library books.
- The banker was upset after he *mislaid* the important documents.

Foresight

Syn – Foreknowledge, forethought, prescience, prudence, presentiment.

eg.

- My parent's *forethought* in the crisis saved us many troubles.
- She had a *presentiment* of danger as soon as she walked into the dark room.

Ant – Shortsightedness.

eg.

- It was his *shortsightedness* that he did not invest in any insurance.

Fright

Syn – Apprehension, anxiety, panic, dread, dismay, foreboding, trepidation, fear, terror.

eg.

- Young students are known to get *anxiety* attacks during exams.
- Carla felt *panic* rising in her when the hooligan closed in on her.

Ant – Tranquility, calmness, coolness, equanimity, placidity, composure.

eg.

- The sages urge us to handle troubles with *equanimity*.
- My teacher's *composure* at all times is quite exemplary.

Fraud

Syn – Deceit, con, scam, deception, swindle, hoax, duplicity, stratagem.

eg.

- The plane was held up for over six hours after a *hoax* bomb call.
- The *deception* of his trusted officer disturbed him.

Ant – Honesty, probity, integrity.

eg.

- *Honesty* is one of the pillars of good character.
- Ramesh's *integrity* was a byword in his business circle.

Frequent

Syn – Recurrent, common, regular, numerous, many, repeated.

eg.

- The trains rushed past at *frequent* intervals.
- Shasti is a *regular* visitor to their house.

Ant - Infrequent, sporadic, uncommon, intermittent, irregular.

eg.

- The doctor told him that he had *irregular* heart-beat.
- The weather forecast says that we can expect *intermittent* showers today.

Fresh

Syn – New, clean, bright, unsullied, brand new.

eg.

- I'll just make some *fresh* coffee for you.
- Manoj took Hira for a drive in his *brand new* car.

Ant - Old, jaded, lackluster.

eg.

- The *old* newspapers were tied with a string.
- She was quite upset about the condition of her *lackluster* hair.

Fuss

Syn – Commotion, excitement, argument, ruckus, protest, upheaval.

eg.

- The customer kicked up a *fuss* when he saw a fly in his soup.
- There was *commotion* in the Parliament when the leader used offens-ive language.

G

Gabble

Syn – Nonsense, twaddle, drivel, baloney, tripe.

eg.

- "Calm down and stop gabbling," scolded my sister. "Tell me what happened."
- The boy talked *drivel* after getting drunk.

Gadget

Syn – Widget, device, imple-ment, tool.

eg.

- He gifted his dad a neat *gadget* for sharpening knives.
- The blood pressure measuring *device* was faulty.

Gag

Syn – Choke, suppress, stifle, curb, restrain, muffle.

eg.

- The fetid smell of the decomposed body made the policeman *gag*.
- She *stifled* a yawn with her hand.

Gain

Syn – Increase, add, grow, expand, get, achieve.

eg.

- Many of the young politician's ideas *gained* popular support.
- The anti-smoking lobby has *increased* the tempo of its campaign in India.

Ant - Lose, drop.

eg.

- The students did not want to *lose* marks due to a printing error.
- Kavya was happy to see that her friend had *dropped* a few kilos.

Game

Syn – Diversion, sport, amusement, match, competition.

eg.

- We used to play indoor *games* like scrabble and carom-board during our summer holidays.

- The boys announced that there would be a cricket *match* on Sunday.

Gang

Syn – Mob, team, squad, crew, group, bunch.

eg.

- The parents denied that their son was ever a *gang* member.
- It was fascinating to watch the cultural program put up by my motley *group* of students.

Gather

Syn – Congregate, group, collect, convene, get together, assemble.

eg.

- The music band *assembled* backstage.
- The little girls got their basket to *collect* flowers.

Ant – Disband, scatter, separate.

eg.

- The wind *scatters* the seed of the plants.
- The rock group *disbanded* when differences between them grew.

Gay

Syn – Cheerful, jovial, happy, cheery, vivacious, jolly, joyous, sprightly, buoyant, blithe.

eg.

- The nursery classroom was painted in *cheerful* colors.

- The children were in a *buoyant* mood after winning the competition.

Ant – Mournful, unhappy, depressed, gloomy, sorrowful, sad, dismal.

eg.

- The day looked *gloomy* with grey skies.
- The painting had a *sad* looking puppy sitting outside his house.

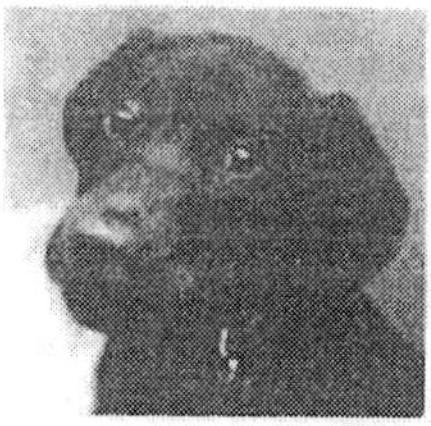

General

Syn – Common, broad, public, universal, accepted.

eg.

- It is a *universal* fact that lack of growth leads to stagnation.
- Swayamvar was an *accepted* norm in ancient India.

Ant – Uncommon, unusual, queer, specific.

eg.

- For mother it was an *unusual* sight to see Parag with books.
- The advertising agency wanted to target *specific* age group.

Generous

Syn – Liberal, lavish, noble, kind, bountiful, giving, munificent, magnanimous.

eg.

- The *magnanimous* king gave gold coins to the poor Brahmin.
- The new government proposed a *liberal* economic policy.

Ant – Niggardly, selfish, greedy, sparing.

eg.

- My boss' *niggardly* ways were a topic of much ridicule.
- The *greedy* son forged his mother's signature on the property papers.

Glorify

Syn – Extol, worship, adore, deify, venerate, exalt, commend, praise.

eg.

- Shaurya *adores* his little sister.
- In the Stone Age, man *deified* nature.

Ant – Abuse, reject, condemn.

eg.

- The warden *condemned* the rowdy behavior of the students.
- Asin hated her father whenever he *abused* her.

Gifted

Syn – Intelligent, able, skilful, exceptional, talented.

eg.

- Meera was an *exceptional* devotee of Lord Krishna.

- The little pianist was extraordinarily *talented*.

Ant – Foolish, stupid, idiotic, stolid.

eg.

- The *foolish* girl talked about her private life with all her friends.
- The drunk had an *idiotic* grin on his face.

Gorgeous

Syn – Stunning, magnificent, beautiful, elegant, dazzling, splendid, grand.

eg.

- The *magnificent* sunset took my breath away.
- The bride looked *stunning* in the bridal outfit.

Ant – Colorless, simple, unadorned, somber.

eg.

- The park was *unadorned* yet looked beautiful.
- Heera's face became *colorless* when she heard about the accident.

Govern

Syn – Rule, run, control, preside over, manage, direct, supervise, administer, command.

eg.

- The head office sent an officer to *manage* the local office.
- Aul *supervised* the construction of his house.

Gradual

Syn – Slow, steady, measured, continuous, regular, progressive.

eg.

- *'Slow* and *steady* wins the race' – said the tortoise.

- The daily wage laborer wanted a *regular* line of work.

Ant – Rapid, momentary, unanticipated, unforeseen.

eg.

- His rise to fame was quite *rapid.*
- There was a *momentary* lull after the speech before the audience started clapping.

Grand

Syn – Noble, lordly, stately, majestic, resplendent, august, superb, exalted, illustrious.

eg.

- The Queen's *stately* mansion is a major tourist attraction.
- His robe was *resplendent* with real gems.

Ant – Inferior, ignoble, dishonorable, shameful.

eg.

- This shop was known for selling *inferior* goods.
- The *dishonorable* incident smeared her reputation forever.

Grief

Syn – Pain, sorrow, heartache, anguish, angst, trouble, affliction, bereavement, distress.

eg.

- Tears give vent to *sorrow.*
- There was *anguish* in the eyes of the little boy as he was led away from his mother.

Ant – Glee, joy contentment, satisfaction, happiness, pleasure.

eg.

- Seeing the ice-cream van, the little girl rubbed her hands in *glee*.

- Money cannot buy *happiness*.

Groundless

Syn – False, unsupported, baseless, unauthorized.

eg.

- The leader gave a statement that the newspaper report was *false* and *baseless*.
- The new theory was *unsupported* facts and figures.

Ant – Actual, well-founded, substantial, positive, real, solid.

eg.

- Arti's fears about the burglar were *real* and *well-founded*.
- The policemen were *positive* that Achyut was the thief they had been looking for.

H

Habit

Syn – Custom, routine, practice, tradition, convention, pattern, tendency.

eg.

- She has a *habit* of twirling her hair when she's thinking.
- It is a *tradition* in his family for all first-born males to get their ears pierced.

Habitat

Syn – Home, surroundings, locale, environment, surroundings, haunt, territory.

eg.

- The grasslands are the natural *habitat* for animals like deer and giraffe.

- Nikhil was *home* for the holidays.

Habitual

Syn – Accustomed, chronic, routine, usual.

eg.

- Varun is *accustomed* to the working style of the US.
- Megha is a *chronic* and compulsive whiner.

Ant – Unaccustomed.

eg.

- Shruti is *unaccustomed* to a working woman's life.

Hack

Syn – Cut, slice, chop, hew, slash, illegal access to computer data.

eg.

- In Uttarakhand, whole forests have been *hacked* down to make way for factories.
- Somebody *hacked* into my company's central database and stole vital information.

Half

Syn – Semi, partially, partly, somewhat.

eg.

- Over *half* the guests had already arrived by seven o' clock.
- I saw Navya standing in front of the mirror, *partly* dressed, applying her makeup.

Ant - Fully, completely, entirely, wholly, totally.

eg.

- Uma was *totally* convinced about the superiority of organic food.
- He took over the running of the company *completely*.

Handy

Syn – Skilful, useful, practical, expert, adroit, usable, versatile, dexterous, close, convenient, proficient, near, ready.

eg.

- The couple sought out the fertility *expert's* advice.
- The department store was very *conveniently* located from my new house.

Ant – Unskilled, unskillful, bungling, clumsy.

eg.

- The *unskilled* laborer is not paid as well as the skilled one.
- My cousin is a *clumsy* person.

Handle

Syn – Hold, wield, touch, grip, knob, lever, switch, carry out.

eg.

- The mechanic turned the *lever* to switch on the machine.
- The old lady *gripped* the handrails firmly.

Hard

Syn – Arduous, difficult, laborious, perplexing, hostile, indisputable, troublesome, trying, firm, solid.

eg.

- The young twins looked angelic, but were quite *troublesome*.

- The witness turned *hostile* after he was threatened.

Ant – Easy, simple, plain.

eg.

- The teacher found it *easy* to handle the junior class.
- '*Simple* living and high thinking' was the motto that Gandhiji lived by.

Harsh

Syn – Jarring, raucous, strident, discordant, cruel, unkind, callous, ruthless.

eg.

- The telephone ring sounded *jarring* in the silence of the movie hall.
- The old man was cold and *callous* towards his children.

Ant – Musical, tuneful, melodious, mild.

eg.

- We enjoyed the *musical* fountains at the Vrindavan Gardens.
- The doctor advised her to use a *mild* shampoo.

Hazard

Syn – Danger, peril, risk, venture, threat, contingency, take a chance (used as 'hazard a guess')

eg.

- The little cub's life was in *danger* in the forest.
- Alice's life was at *peril* in the Queen's land.

Ant – Assurance, certainty, protection, safeguard, security.

eg.

- The bank wanted some *security* against the loan.
- The manager's *assurance* that the loan would be passed was enough for Rajesh.

Healthy

Syn – Vigorous, fit, sound, hale and hearty, well, strong, robust.

eg.

- The elderly gentleman looked *hale and hearty.*

- Suman felt *strong* after drinking the chicken soup.

Ant – Sickly, ill, unhealthy, weak, weakly, unsound, sick.

eg.

- The pup looked *sickly* and *weak.*
- The children took *ill* after eating food from the canteen.

Hesitate

Syn – Waver, pause, falter, vacillate, demur, dither, shilly-shally.

eg.

- The manager *wavered* for a minute before handing Manav his pink slip.
- The cricket star tried to *shilly-shally* instead of giving a direct reply.

Ant – Determine, settle, end, decide, resolve.

eg.

- Shalini was *determined* to lose weight.
- The conflict was *resolved* amicably between the two brothers.

Heavy

Syn – Crushing, burdensome, onerous, oppressive, serious, grave, important, deep, profound.

eg.

- The management discussed the *serious* issues at hand.
- Gia found the metaphysics class very *profound* but dull.

Ant – Trivial, easy, light, mild.

eg.

- Bindi tried to make the atmosphere *light* by cracking jokes.
- The friends talked about *trivial* matters when they met after a long time.

Highest

Syn – Topmost, uppermost, supreme, maximum, peak, chief, main, top, premier.

eg.

- The climbers rested for a while before starting the ascent to reach the *peak*.
- My father's health was the *uppermost* concern in my mind.

Ant – Undermost, lowest, deepest, bottom.

eg.

- His business hit rock *bottom* during recession.
- Charan's self-esteem was at its *lowest* after his divorce.

Holy

Syn – Religious, sacred, consecrated, godly, divine, saintly, hallowed, sanctified.

eg.

- The teacher had a *saintly* expression on her face.
- The little child was not interested in the *religious* ceremony.

Ant – Irreligious, ungodly, irreverent, sacrilegious, profane.

eg.

- The young are *irreverent* by nature.
- Ravan committed the *irreligious* act of kidnapping another man's wife.

Horrible

Syn – Frightful, terrible, nasty, appalling, ghastly,

fearful, dreadful, awful, hideous, repulsive, ugly.

eg.

- The ghetto looked and smelled *awful*.
- The man's face was covered with *hideous* pock marks.

Ant – Agreeable, pleasant, delightful, pleasurable, charming, pleasing.

eg.

- The girl's smile was very *pleasant*
- Dimple has a *charming* face.

Hot

Syn – Burning, boiling, blistering, feverish, scorching, sizzling, searing, torrid.

eg.

- The *blistering* heat left us exhausted.
- The old man was feeling *feverish*.

Ant – Cold, calm, cool, soothing.

eg.

- Ira tried to *calm* her mind before going for the interview.
- The little baby's mother sang a *soothing* lullaby.

Humble

Syn – Modest, unassuming, retiring, meek.

eg.

- Despite his stupendous achievements, Nobel Laureate Amartya Sen remains a *modest* and *unassuming* man.

- The business tycoon rose from *humble* beginnings to become the boss of an international conglomerate.

Ant - Arrogant, conceited, supercilious, haughty, proud.

eg.

- The *haughty* duchess punished the slave girl for a small mistake.
- Kshama is the most *conceited* and selfish person I have ever known.

Humid

Syn – Wet, moist, damp, sticky, clammy, muggy, sultry, oppressive.

eg.

- The day was so *sultry* that we decided not to go and play outside.
- The boy's *clammy* hands clung to his mother.

Ant – Parched, dry, arid.

eg.

- My throat felt *parched* on the hot day.
- The clothes were left to *dry* on the clothes line.

Humourous

Syn – Funny, witty, amusing, hilarious, comic, droll, jocose, jocular.

eg.

- The *hilarious* movie improved our mood.
- The *witty* dialogue between the hero and heroine were the highlight of the movie.

Ant – Serious, grave, dull, sedate, gloomy.

eg.

- To compensate for the *dull* evening, Ramona decided to go to the discotheque.
- The abandoned house looked *gloomy* and forlorn.

I

Idea

Syn – Thought, scheme, plan, design, initiative, inspira-tion.

eg.

- Lately I've been toying with the *idea* of going back to college.
- The *thought* behind taking tuitions was to save money.

Ideal

Syn – Archetype, model, perfect, idyllic, prototype, example.

eg.

- Lisa enjoyed a *perfect* holiday in Egypt.

- Goa is an *idyllic* holiday spot for tourists.

Ant – Factual, realistic, practical.

eg.

- Kareem's paintings are quite *realistic.*
- Her live-in cook is a driver also for all *prac-tical* purposes.

Identical

Syn – Same, equivalent, ditto, tantamount, alike, similar.

eg.

- Aisha and Tia talk and dress *alike*.
- My dress is *similar* to the one which I saw in the magazine.

Ant – Different, unlike.

eg.

- The twins are as *different* from each other as chalk from cheese.
- The job turned out to be quite *unlike* what he had expected.

Idle

Syn – Inert, redundant, unoccupied, lazy, still, inactive, slothful, sluggish, unemployed, indolent.

eg.

- The old man felt *sluggish* and tired all the time.
- Aslam was *unemployed* for a long time.

Ant – Active, busy, diligent, industrious, assiduous.

eg.

- The best way to be healthy is to stay *active.*
- Sarthak is very *diligent* in his work.

Ignore

Syn – Overlook, disregard, discount.

eg.

- The phone rang, but she *ignored* it.
- The teacher tried to *overlook* the student's behavior.

Imitate

Syn – Burlesque, echo, emulate, duplicate, follow, replicate, copy, impersonate, mimic, forge.

eg.

- So many times it is difficult to tell whether art *mimics* life, or vise versa.
- The official was suspended for *impersonating* his superior.

Improve

Syn – Amend, reform, rectify, correct, ameliorate, better, increase, progress, advance, develop, recover, perk up.

eg.

- The examiner did not let him *rectify* the mistake.
- Her aim was to make *amends* with the sibling she had hurt so often in the past.

Ant – Spoil, deteriorate, corrupt, mar, impair, pollute, damage, rot.

eg.

- Latifah *spoilt* the effect of the dress by over accessorizing.
- The patient's health *deteriorated* rapidly.

Incapable

Syn – Incompetent, inefficient, inept, unqualified, inadequate, unable, helpless, unfit.

eg.

- Ajay was declared medically *unfit* for the job.
- Sana fired her *incompetent* chauffeur.

Ant – Gifted, capable, qualified, accomplished, competent, efficient.

eg.

- The company wanted to hire a *qualified* accountant.
- The dentist was looking for a *competent* secretary.

Inclement

Syn – Rough, stormy, rainy, unfavorable, windy, foul, unpleasant.

eg.

- The ship had to navigate through *stormy* seas in *rough* weather.
- The day was *windy* and *unfavorable* for kite flying.

Ant – Genial, mild, favorable, pleasant.

eg.

- The *mild* summer evening air was rich with the fragrance of flowers.
- The captain announced that the wind was *favorable* for sailing.

Incline

Syn – Dispose, predispose, persuade, prejudice, bias, lean, fall upon, tend towards, slant, slope.

eg.

- Gender *bias* has an undeniable presence in our modern society.

- Politically speaking, Margaret *leans* towards the Left.

Ant – Put off, rise, go upwards, repel.

eg.

- The high *rise* building looked majestic against the skyline.
- Sharon was *put off* by her boyfriend's sweaty smell.

Include

Syn – Involve, possess, comprise, contain.

eg.

- This book *comprises* of word meanings and their opposites.
- "This encyclopedia contains enough information for your project," his mother said.

Ant – Exclude, omit, leave out.

eg.

- The police *excluded* the possibility of forced entry into the victim's house.
- Mayank *omitted* to mention the nature of his business visit to his wife.

Incongruous

Syn – Inconsistent, unfit, out of place, strange, bizarre, inappropriate, absurd, incompatible.

eg.

- It was *inappropriate* on the manager's part to comment on the dress of a guest.
- I felt *out of place* at my friend's family get-together.

Ant – Congruous, agreeable, appropriate, in agreement.

eg.

- My new friend and I found that we were *in agreement* on most issues.
- It seemed *appropriate* that Jessica's sister be her bridesmaid.

Inconsiderate

Syn – Heedless, indifferent, intolerant, rash, hasty, selfish, thoughtless, uncaring, unkind.

eg.

- My boss is *selfish*, and only concerned about meeting his deadlines and targets.
- Thenny's *unkind* words brought tears to her friend's eyes.

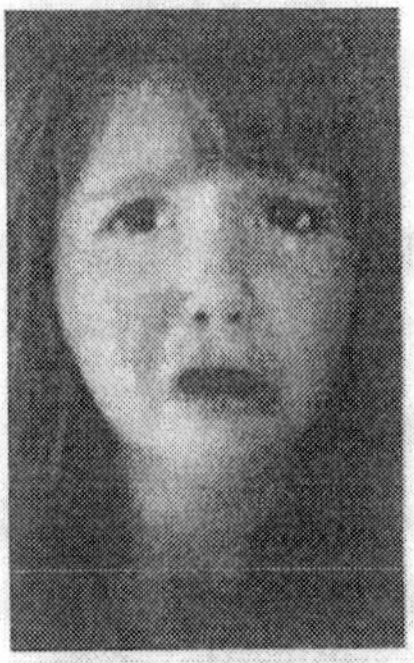

Ant – Considerate, heedful.

eg.

- The new professor was extremely *considerate* about the weak students.
- The matron was *heedful* of the nutritional demands of growing teenagers.

Inconstant

Syn – Variable, changeable, fluctuating, irregular, fickle, erratic, mercurial, varying.

eg.

- The *fluctuating* share index has flummoxed the shareholders.
- The *fickle* minded girl could not decide which dress to wear.

Ant – Constant, steadfast, fixed.

eg.

- To the young widow, her child was a *constant* reminder of his dead father.
- The dog remained *fixed* to the spot long after his mistress disappeared out of sight.

Incur

Syn – Meet, lay yourself open to, invite, acquire, earn, deserve, sustain, blame.

eg.

- The host *invited* a limited number of guests.

- Keshav's father *blamed* his friends for his poor marks.

Ant – Shun, avoid, escape, defect.

eg.

- Garima *shuns* the company of her ill-behaved classmates.
- Nakul *avoids* any discussion about his fut ure.

Indecent

Syn – Shameless, lewd, offensive, coarse, rude, impolite, indelicate, indecorous, improper, filthy, foul, unchaste.

eg.

- The boys passed *lewd* comments and whistled at the girls.
- The reporter had to issue an apology for his *offensive* article about the big star.

Ant – Decent, decorous, pure, moral, virtuous, seemly, proper, chaste.

eg.

- Sita was a *virtuous* wife.

- The little girl looked prim and *proper.*

Induce

Syn – Impel, persuade, encourage, tempt, cajole, urge, coax, wheedle, move.

eg.

- His own motivation to reach the top *impelled* him on.
- Abha was *tempted* to buy the new Cadbury chocolate.

Ant – Hinder, repel, discourage, subdue.

eg.

- Similar poles of a magnet *repel.*
- My mother *discouraged* me from learning swimming.

Influence

Syn – Actuate, draw, excite, incline, lead, prompt, urge, move, induce, stir, incite, compel, drive, inflame.

eg.

- When Karan was giving his exam he heard someone *prompt* from behind his seat.
- If you stay even a day with my dog he will *drive* you nuts.

Ant – Dissuade, hinder, deter, prevent, inhibit, restrain.

eg.

- Rajni *dissuaded* her brother from joining the army.
- It is better to *prevent* a disease rather than run around to the doctors to cure it.

Inner

Syn – Inward, inside, central, interior, middle, private, personal, internal, real.

eg.

- The *central* courtyard of the house had fresh air and sunlight.
- The shaded area *inside* the jungle was cold and dark.

Ant – Outer, exterior, external, superficial.

eg.

- Myna suffered *superficial* burns on her hands.
- Our armed forces look after both internal and *external* security.

Innocent

Syn – Blameless, sinless, untainted, naïve, virginal, not guilty, irreproachable.

eg.

- Red Riding Hood was *naïve* enough to think that the wolf wouldn't eat her.

- The minister prided herself on her *untainted* reputation.

Ant – Blameworthy, culpable, guilty, immoral, lewd, impure, unchaste, depraved, dirty, indecent.

eg.

- The man confessed having *impure* thoughts about his brother's wife.
- Fiza was *guilty* of eating the whole box of chocolates.

Insolence

Syn – Rudeness, impertinence, contempt, disrespect, insult, insubordination.

eg.

- Maya could not tolerate *disrespect* from her family.
- The students had no intention of *insulting* the staff members.

Ant – Deference, regard.

eg.

- The entire clan shows due *deference* to the old patriarch.
- Paul had the highest *regard* for his brother.

Insolvent

Syn – Bankrupt, impecunious, broke, in debt.

eg.

- The firm declared itself *bankrupt*.
- The young friends were *broke* and *in debt*.

Ant – Solvent.

eg.

- It was enough to break even and stay *solvent* when the business had just started.

Interity

Syn – Honesty, probity, sincerity, truth, honor, veracity, uprightness.

eg.

- The motto of our academy was *truth* and *honor*.
- *Honesty* is the best policy.

Ant – Unfairness, dishonesty.

eg.

- It was the *unfairness* of the situation which hurt Rose more than the punishment.
- The Khans fired their servant because of his *dishonesty*.

Intimidate

Syn – Bully, daunt, frighten, dismay, overawe, terrorize.

eg.

- The idea of attending the rich nobleman's high class party did not *daunt* him at all.
- I was *overawed* by the majestic sunset.

Ant – Encourage, comfort, assuage.

eg.

- Shirin *encouraged* her little puppy to step out of his kennel.
- The nurse tried to *comfort* the patient's family.

J

Jabber

Syn – Chatter, talk, prattle, gabble, idle chat.

eg.

- I listened to the children's *chatter* and wondered what they were talking.
- The little baby's *prattle* cheered the mother.

Ant – Reticence, silence.

eg.

- The defendant's *reticence* was mistaken for admission of guilt.
- There was *silence* in the woods.

Jarring

Syn – Harsh, loud, grating, strident, raucous, scratchy.

eg.

- The glass cutter made a *grating* sound.
- The *strident* ringing of the telephone disturbed her sleep.

Ant – Soothing, musical.

eg.

- The pianist played a *soothing* tune.

- The Broadway is a very famous *musical* show in America.

Jealous

Syn – Envious, green eyed, covetous, desirous, invidious.

eg.

- My friend is very *envious* of my academic grades.
- Amy was *green eyed* with jealousy when I got a new car.

Jest

Syn – Joke, fun, jeer, taunt, amuse.

eg.

- I was very *amused* to see my pictures of the kindergarten days.
- Jugal doesn't like it when my friends joke about him.

Ant – Seriousness, thoughtful, earnest, sober.

eg.

- It was very *thoughtful* of my friend to call me after so many years for my birthday.
- The driver had to assure the policeman that he was *sober*.

Jibe

Syn – Taunt, dig, sneer, crack.

eg.

- Her stepmother's *taunts* her all the time.
- Vir disliked the *dig* his friends made about his father's business.

Ant – Praise, extol.

eg.

- Rohan *praised* the captain's performance in the match.
- Macy *extolled* the student's efforts.

Joyous

Syn – Ecstatic, elated, jovial, merry, blissful, festive, genial, jolly, glad, happy.

eg.

- Lynn's mother was very *happy* to see her grades.
- Sanya enjoyed the *festive* season of Goa.

Ant – Morose, gloomy, miserable, solemn, sad, unhappy.

eg.

- The little boy looked *solemn* as he sat in the school bus.

- The clerk looked *morose* as he sat doing his boring paperwork.

Justify

Syn – Absolve, defend, clear, validate, rationalize, ex-plain, excuse.

eg.

- Jay tried to *defend* himself when the teacher accused him of cheating.
- The accused was *absolved* of all the charges.

Ant – Condemn, accuse, censure, blame, denounce.

eg.

- Patel *accused* his friend of stealing his book.
- Khushi feared her mother's *censure* about her dress.

K

Kaput

Syn – Broken, ruined, wrecked, finished, ended, useless, defunct.

eg.

- The new TV has gone *kaput*.
- Vinny's new boat was *wrecked* in the accident.

Keen

Syn – Acute, eager, sharp, fanatical, intense, enthusiastic, shrewd, penetrating.

eg.

- Aruna was *eager* to join the course.
- Shraddha was very *enthusiastic* about sports.

Ant – Slow, stupid, bland, languid, dull, indifferent.

eg.

- Trish's younger brother was *slow* and *stupid*.
- It is not nice to be *indifferent* to the wishes of one's employees.

Keep

Syn – Stay, be, remain, maintain, continue, go on.

eg.

- My cousin is going to *stay* with me when she comes to India.
- The Taj Mahal *remains* a wonder of the world even today.

Ant – Discard, destroy.

eg.

- Our school authorities advice us to *destroy* plastic bottles after use.
- The professor *discarded* the old unused files.

Kill

Syn – Assassinate, massacre, murder, slaughter, slay, execute, butcher, dispatch, put to death.

eg.

- The plan to *assassinate* the President was masterminded by a terrorist group.
- The Jallianwala Bagh *massacre* was a turning point in the freedom movement of India.

Ant – Create, produce, fashion, cause, originate.

Kind

Syn – Compassionate, benign, affable, generous, lenient, sympathetic, charitable, merciful, tender, philanthropic, complacent, type, class, sort, variety, brand, category.

eg.

- Our English teacher is very *lenient*.
- The girls in my *class* are very fond of reading books.

Ant – Cruel, callous, unfeeling, unkind, hard-hearted, insensible, harsh.

eg.

- The *cruel* king killed his brothers.
- The *unfeeling* stepmother asked their father to leave Hansel and Gretel in the forest.

Kindle

Syn – Ignite, inflame, light, fire up, encourage, stimulate, inspire, rouse.

eg.

- The fiery speech *inflamed* the workers.

- Stories *fire up* a child's imagination.

Ant – Extinguish, put out, satisfy, satiate.

eg.

- Karan tried to *extinguish* the fire in his room.
- Mother *put out* the lamp when it was time for us to sleep.

Knock

Synonyms - Bang, thump, thud, rap, tap, blow, beat (used as 'knock out'), hammer.

eg.

- The children *knocked* at the door, but no one opened.
- Shruti *banged* her head against the glass door.

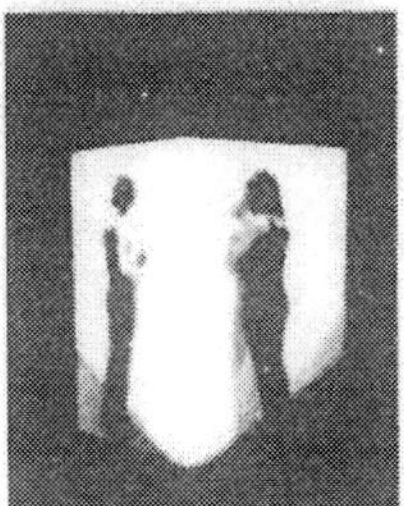

Know

Syn – Recognize, identify, discern, distinguish, have information.

eg.

- There are instructions in the manual telling you everything you need to *know*.
- Eva recognized a good thing when she saw it, so she took another helping of the pudding.

Knowledge

Syn – Perception, science, wisdom, intuition, comprehension, information, cognition, lore, light, learning, erudition, intelligence.

eg.

- Keira's charming manners and *intelligence* made her an interesting companion.
- Mariam is keen on *learning* a new language.

Ant – Ignorance, unfamiliarity, misunderstanding,

misapprehension, inexperience, illiteracy.

eg.

- His *ignorance* about the gravity of the situation landed him in trouble.
- There was a *misunderstanding* between the two friends after which they did not speak to each other.

L

Label

Syn – Tag, sticker, marker, brand.

eg.

- Fancy designer *labels* come with even fancier price *tags* to match.
- The media had unnecessarily *branded* him as a troublemaker.

Labour

Syn – Work, toil, exertion, drudgery, grind, industry, childbirth, delivery.

eg.

- The *exertion* of his work showed on his face.
- It was the *drudgery* of everyday existence which was killing the artist's creativity.

Ant – Repose, rest, relaxation, stillness.

eg.

- The doctor advised Mohan to take a good diet and complete *rest*.
- Deep breathing leads to *relaxation*.

Lack

Syn – Need, shortage, deficiency, require, want.

eg.

- There was *shortage* of rice this year due to poor rainfall.
- Rickets is caused due to *deficiency* of Vitamin D.

Ant – Sufficiency, prosperity, wealth, riches.

eg.

- India saw a period of peace and *prosperity* under the Gupta rulers.

- Good health is the true *wealth.*

Large

Syn – Big, mammoth, great, bulky, hefty, huge, fat, monumental.

eg.

- The *mammoth* building looked quite an eyesore.
- The *bulky* package came by post.

Ant – Small, minute, delicate.

eg.

- The *delicate* sapling wilted in the sun.
- The *small* girl was frightened of the dark.

Lawful

Syn – Rightful, legal, fair, official, endorsed, legitimate.

eg.

- The *legal* matter was pending in the court.
- The *official* inaugural ceremony before the Olympics was marked by pomp and splendor.

Ant – Illegal, unlawful, illicit.

eg.

- Girish was arrested for being involved in *illegal* trade of arms.
- Tanmay admitted having *illicit* relations with his friend's wife.

Lazy

Syn – Idle, sluggish, indolent, unemployed, lethargic, languid, slow, slothful.

eg.

- Basant feels *sluggish* in the afternoons.
- The friends talked about how they dreaded being *unemployed* after college.

Ant – Active, energetic, agile, up and doing.

eg.

- The little pup was very healthy and *active.*
- The girl playing basketall was quite *energetic.*

Leader

Syn – Guide, chief, head, manager, director, conductor, principal, politician.

eg.

- Pranab is the new *head* of the department.
- The young *politician* was welcomed on his first day in the Parliament by the old-timers.

Ant – Follower, trainee, apprentice, pupil, henchman.

eg.

- The *followers* of Jainism practice Ahimsa or non-violence.
- Stuti is working as an *apprentice* with her father.

Lean

Syn – Bend, incline, tip, slant, thin, slender.

eg.

- Tarun said to his mother, "Do not to watch the speedometer, just *lean* back and enjoy the ride."
- His brother was *lean*, but not *thin*.

Learn

Syn – Acquire, study, find out, hear, memorize, discover, detect, trace.

eg.

- Hira wants to send her son to *study* abroad.
- Julie *memorized* her lines of the school play.

Ant – Forget, unlearn, miss, misunderstand, ignore.

eg.

- Mother asked me not to *forget* to carry out the garbage.
- The doctor asked him not to *ignore* the symptoms.

Lengthy

Syn – Tedious, long, drawn out, prolonged, extensive, diffused, detailed, spread.

eg.

- The director was impatient because the shot was taking really *long*.
- The legal proceedings tend to be *tedious* and *drawn out*.

Ant – Short, concise, brief.

eg.

- The report was *concise* but lucid.
- The teacher asked me to make the introductory speech *brief* and interesting.

Lessen

Syn – Lighten, diminish, decrease, reduce, assuage, allay, mitigate, soften.

eg.

- The doctor told Helen that the size of her fibroid had *reduced.*
- The soothing lullaby *allayed* the little baby's fears.

Ant – Heighten, toughen, enlarge, escalate, extend, intensify.

eg.

- The loudspeakers *intensified* the sound.
- The real estate prices have *escalated* in the last six months or so.

Liberal

Syn – Plentiful, tolerant, profuse, free, moderate.

eg.

- All religions tell us to be *tolerant.*
- India finally became *free* once again on 15th Aug 1947

Ant – Scanty, grasping, mean, low.

eg.

- This year the rainfall was very *scanty.*

Liberty

Syn – Emancipation, freedom, autonomy, independence, license, permission.

eg.

- Our democracy gives us *freedom* of thought, speech and expression.
- I enjoyed my *independence* in the hostel.

Ant – Captivity, compulsion, constraint, imprisonment, slavery, serfdom, servitude, oppression, suppression.

eg.

- The feudal lords of the Middle Ages were notorious for their *oppression* of the slaves.

- The bird in *captivity* does not sing half as good as the bird in the woods.

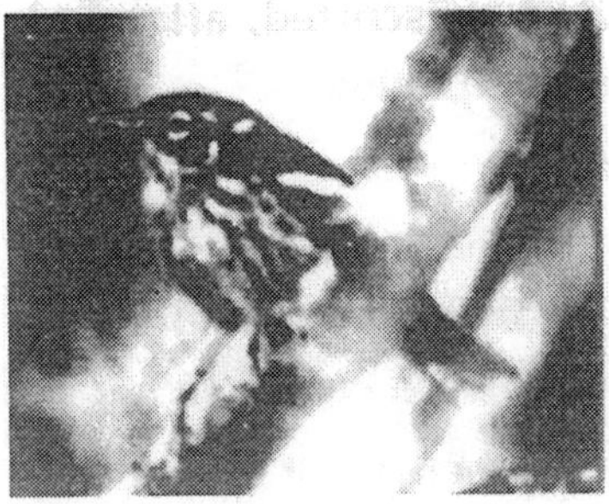

Lift

Syn – Exalt, pick up, haul up, erect, raise, elevate, hoist, boost, steal, pinch, plagiarize.

eg.

- The engineers used big machines to *haul up* the construction material.
- The famous award winning author was sued for *plagiarizing*.

Ant – Drop, lower, sink, let fall.

eg.

- The terrorists *dropped* a bomb on the tallest building.
- The ill-fated ship was doomed to *sink*.

Likely

Syn – Apt, probable, expected, reasonable, liable, credible, possible, conceivable, presumable.

eg.

- It is quite *probable* that the weatherman's prediction turns out to be wrong.
- The famous card shop has a card for every *conceivable* occasion.

Ant – Doubtful, improbable, questionable, unlikely, dubious, unreasonable.

eg.

- It is wrong of parents to have *unreasonable* expectations from their children.
- It seemed *unlikely* that mother would return before noon from her office.

Lively

Syn – Vivid, dynamic, bubbly, animated, energetic, sparkling, brisk, keen, vivacious, spirited.

eg.

- The *spirited* young foal would have to be broken in before he'd let anyone ride him.

- The old man was immensely cheered up by the visit of her *bubbly* young granddaughter.

Ant – Listless, languid, lethargic, languorous.

eg.

- The dog felt *lethargic* on the hot summer afternoon.
- Shravan felt *listless* and sad after his friend left town.

Lonely

Syn – Solitary, lonesome, forlorn, lost, alone.

eg.

- The puppy looked *lost* and *forlorn* without its master.
- Manvi felt *lonesome* when her husband went out on a tour.

Ant – Escorted, attended, accompanied.

eg.

- The big star was *escorted* by her boyfriend for the award ceremony.
- Neeta went to the party *accompanied* by her mother.

Look

Syn – Behold, inspect, see, watch, stare, gaze, observe, regard, survey, view, discern, seem, appear.

eg.

- Jagat likes to *gaze* at the stars in the night sky.
- Things are not always what they *seem*.

Ant – Ignorance, reject, veil, bypass.

eg.

- When it comes to one's health, *ignorance* is certainly not bliss.

- The young bride's face was half covered with a *veil*.

Love

Syn – Affection, fondness, adore, liking, regard, friendship, tenderness, attraction.

eg.

- Juliet's *affection* for her brother was there for all to see.
- The young brothers held Yudhishtra in the highest *regard*.

Ant – Dislike, abhorrence, animosity, disgust, repugnance, antipathy, abomination, loathing, aversion, detestation.

eg.

- Mia *disliked* the rigid rules and discipline of the hostel.
- I have an *aversion* for scheming and conniving women.

Luck

Syn – Fortune, chance, fate, destiny, providence, prosperity, good stroke.

eg.

- *Fortune* is the fickle goddess which bestows and withdraws without any apparent reason.
- It was pure *chance* that they won the lottery.

Ant – Bad luck, misfortune, bad stroke, unfavorable.

eg.

- *Bad luck* continued to bring more trouble to the big rice company.
- It was Akshat's *misfortune* that his mother saw him on the only day he bunked class.

Lump

Syn – Swelling, knob, bulge, protuberance, piece, chunk.

eg.

- She had to strain the custard to remove the *lumps*.

- The *swelling* on her hand subsided after a week.

Lure

Syn – Entice, tempt, decoy, attract, allure, bait.

eg.

- Computers are *luring* the young away from outdoor games.
- Punit was inexperienced enough not to be *tempted* by the wily young woman.

Ant - Repel, dislike.

eg.

- Like poles, we can see, *repel*, and unlike poles attract.
- I *dislike* the whole idea of misleading advertisements.

Lurk

Syn – Prowl, loiter, skulk, wait, hang around.

eg.

- She didn't see the figure *lurking* behind the bushes.
- The boys loitered aimlessly in the deserted hallway of their college.

Lust

Syn – Yearn, desire, covet, long for.

eg.

- She had secretly *lusted* after her brother in law for years.
- He *longed for* freedom to make his own career decisions.

Luxuriant

Syn – Abundant, plentiful, copious, ample, lush, flourishing.

eg.

- The film's *luxuriant* visuals made it a delight to watch it on full screen.
- The *plentiful* crop ensured a smooth year for the farmers.

Ant - Meager, paltry, skimpy, scanty.

eg.

- He had to make both ends meet on his *meager* salary.
- The young girl wore a *skimpy* swimming suit.

M

Macabre

Syn – Ghoulish, grisly, ghastly, chilling, morbid, gruesome.

eg.

- The twin murders told a *macabre* tale of lust and greed.
- He has a *morbid* sense of humour.

Machine

Syn – Engine, appliance, apparatus, equipment, tool, gadget, device.

eg.

- The fax *machine* is not working properly.
- The *engine* of my car was making a strange sound.

Macro

Syn – International, total, universal, comprehensive, overall.

eg.

- My *macro*-economics paper deals with the US economy.
- She has done a *comprehensive* course on reflexology.

Ant - Micro.

eg.

- She asked her brother to get a *micro* computer from the US.

Mad

Syn – Foolish, crazy, barmy, nutty, foolish, silly, unbalanced, loony, insane, distraught, angry, zany, zealous.

eg.

- The *zealous* followers took out a protest march.
- The *silly* girl fought with her best friend.

Ant – Sane, genius, calm, intelligent.

eg.

- The woman stayed *calm* even in the crisis.
- Arun is an *intelligent* man.

Magnanimous

Syn – Generous, fair-minded, noble, worthy, honorable, upright.

eg.

- The king was *generous* to a fault.
- The *noble* woman gave alms to the poor woman.

Ant – Mean, selfish.

eg.

- Lanny is a *mean* friend.
- Raunaq is not a *selfish* boy.

Majestic

Syn – Regal, royal, grand, stately, imposing, grandiose, magnificent, splendid.

eg.

- The high tea at the embassy was a *splendid* affair.
- The *regal* old lady was giving orders to her servants.

Ant – Coarse, crude.

eg.

- The laborer had calluses on his *coarse* palms.
- The language of the farmers was very *crude.*

Majority

Syn – Adulthood, excess, superiority, bulk, mass, popular, common, preponderance.

eg.

- Lack of concentration is a *common* problem with students.
- The heavy books added to the *bulk* of the child's school bag.

Ant – Minority, smallness, inferiority.

eg.

- The government has opposed the reservation for the *minority* classes.

- The middle aged woman felt a sense of *inferiority* among the younger lot.

Manner

Syn – Style, mode, custom, method, system, way, fashion, conduct, behavior.

eg.

- The new student's retro dressing *style* was the butt of everybody's jokes.
- Himani's *behavior* seemed loud and quite out of place.

Ant – Discourteous, unsocial, unsystematic, unmethodical.

eg.

- The *discourteous* child was summoned to the principal's room.
- Ratan's work is quite *unsystematic.*

Melody

Syn – Unison, tune, music, harmony, air, symphony.

eg.

- Shubhi enjoyed the lyrical *tune* which was being played on the radio.
- The orchestra was playing Beethoven's *symphony.*

Ant – Discordant, distortion, disruption, noise.

eg.

- The pianist tried to fix the *discordant* notes in his piece.
- The traffic *noise* kept us awake all night.

Mercy

Syn – Benevolence, favor, pardon, clemency, compassion, leniency, pity, gentleness, mildness, grace, kindness.

eg.

- The convict begged for *clemency* from the judge.
- The teacher decided to deal with the truant child with *compassion.*

Ant – Cruelty, harshness, hardness, vigor, severity, penalty, punishment.

eg.

- The *harshness* in mother's tone elicited a quick response from my brother.

- Jaikishan did not approve of the police *cruelty* methods.

Merit

Syn – Worth, value, advantage, excellence, virtue.

eg.

- I *value* the old-fashioned qualities of honesty and integrity.
- Qualified professionals definitely have the competitive *advantage* over their unqualified counterparts.

Ant – Fault, error, flaw, weakness, worthlessness.

eg.

- The characters in Greek mythology usually had one fatal *flaw* which ultimately led to their downfall.
- Sita was punished for no *fault* of hers.

Middle

Syn – Heart, focus, hub, core, center, central point.

eg.

- The *core* of the apple was rotten.
- My department is the *hub* of all commercial activity in my company.

Ant - Outer, periphery, external.

eg.

- The green hedge on the *periphery* of the complex made it look beautiful.
- The External Affairs Minister concluded the peace talks with his Pakistan counterpart.

Might

Syn – Strength, capacity, valour, possibility, permission.

eg.

- I *might* be a few minutes late for the meeting.
- He swung the hammer with all his *might*.

Mild

Syn – Bland, calm, serene, soft, gentle, kind, docile, tender, meek, placid.

eg.

- The *gentle* touch of the nurse's hand soothed the ailing man.
- The *mild* spring evening was fragrant with myriad scents.

Ant – Wild, ferocious, blood-thirsty, fierce, brutish, savage.

eg.

- The *ferocious* looking dog pounced on the milkman.
- Jack the Ripper was a *savage* killer.

Minister

Syn – Brother, monk, pastor, preacher, priest, care, attend, look after.

eg.

- The *pastor* gave the most interesting sermon.
- Rukmini decided to *look after* her aging mother in law herself.

Miscellaneous

Syn – Assorted, mingled, motley, unlike, various.

eg.

- Julia loved the box of *assorted* cookies.
- Our club has a *motley* crowd of members.

Ant – Homogeneous, identical, like, pure, uniform, same, similar.

eg.

- The twins were *like* peas in a pod.
- My friend and I share *similar* interests.

Mischievous

Syn – Naughty, impish, playful, roguish, prankster, playful.

eg.

- The *playful* dwarves tripped and danced around the princess.

- Alan smiled his *roguish* smile when he was caught with his hand in the cookie jar.

Ant – Well behaved, serious, sober.

eg.

- Mrs Baig's little ones are usually very *well behaved*.
- Mother admonished my sister to be more *serious* about her studies.

Mislead

Syn – Misguide, deceive, delude, beguile, misdirect.

eg.

- Some advertisements do tend to *misguide*.
- The nubile girl was *deceived* by the wily man.

Ant – Pilot, guide, direct, steer, lead.

eg.

- The pole star *guides* sailors at sea.
- Neeraj vowed to *steer* clear of trouble in the near future.

Modest

Syn – Lowly, humble, shy, self effacing, meek, reticent, unassuming, unpretentious.

eg.

- The young man was shy and *reticent*.
- Sunehri is an *unassuming* young girl.

Ant – Conceited, pretentious, showy, over-bearing, immodest.

eg.

- The whole wedding affair was *showy* and ostentatious.
- Demi is a *conceited* young girl.

Muscle

Syn – Power, influence, force, might.

eg.

- The doctor asked her to relax her stomach *muscles*.
- The gangster used *force* to extract money illegally.

Must

Syn – Have to, obliged to, ought to, should.

eg.

- All drivers *must* wear seat belts for their own safety.

- You *ought to* visit your parents in the holidays.

Mystery

Syn – Secrecy, obscurity, magueness, enigma.

eg.

- What happened to the body remains a *mystery* till today.
- The actress was an *enigma.*

Myth

Syn – Legend, fable, saga, parable, allegory.

eg.

- The *parables* from Bible teach important moral lessons.
- *Legend* has it that Lord Shiva could destroy the world with his third eye.

N

Nag

Syn – Badger, plague, pester, harass, harry.

eg.

- My mother keeps *naggi-ng* me about my weight.
- Timothy *pestered* his father to go out and play ball with him.

Nail

Syn – Pin, tack, spike, fix, peg, fasten, attach.

eg.

- The key was hanging on a *nail* in the lobby.
- He hammered a *nail* to *fasten* the cupboard in place.

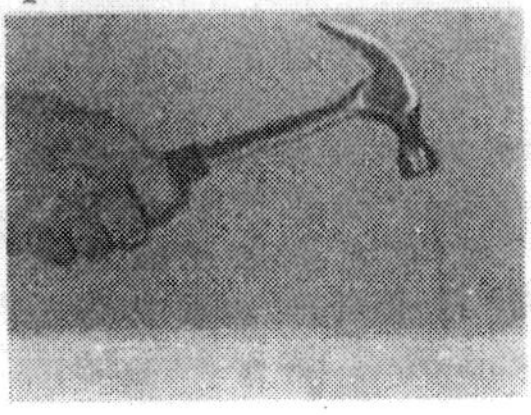

Naïve

Syn – Inexperienced, raw, green, innocent, immature, youthful.

eg.

- She was *naïve* enough to believe every word her boyfriend said to her.
- The young carpenter seemed quite *inexperi-enced.*

Ant - Experienced, mature.

eg.

- The politician was quite *experienced* in pulling the right strings.
- Jenny wanted her husband to deal the tragedy in a more *mature* way.

Name

Syn – Person's name, sur-name, reputation.

eg.
- "Can I have your *surname*?" asked the new teacher.
- He has made a *name* for himself in the field of music.

Narrow

Syn – Thin, slender, slight, contracted, tapered.

eg.
- The stairs leading to my room were very *narrow*.
- He was shaken by his *narrow* escape from death.

Ant - Broad, wide, large, extensive, open.

eg.
- We went along a *broad* passage to the hallway.
- The dentist asked her to open her mouth *wide* open.

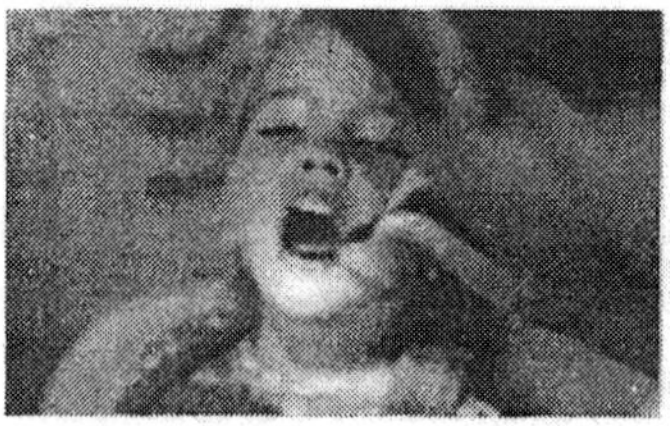

Nasty

Syn – Spiteful, mean, vicious, cruel, horrible, malevolent.

eg.
- The tennis champion was quite upset to read the *nasty* things that were being written about her.
- I know her since the day I got married – she has always been *vicious*.

Native

Syn – Aboriginals, inhabitant, local, innate, natural, natal, national, citizen, original, indigenous.

eg.
- The band played "Jana Gana Mana..." our *national* anthem.
- Khadi is our *indigenous* product.

Ant – Foreign, extraneous, alien, acquired, extrinsic.

eg.
- When one is visiting *foreign* lands, one must respect their culture.
- In the school fancy dress competition, Shaina was dressed like an *alien*.

Necessary

Syn – Essential, crucial, needful, compulsory, required, requisite, undeniable, unavoidable.

eg.

- "This job doesn't *require* any special skills," said the manager.
- English language is *compulsory* in schools here.

Ant – Casual, worthless, non-essential, optional, unnecessary, useless.

eg.

- It was *useless* trying to convince Kiran to dress conservatively.
- Our school principal thinks that giving homework is totally *unnecessary*.

Neglect

Syn – Carelessness, abandon, negligence, omission, oversight, heedlessness, ignore, default, failure, disregard, disrespect, inadvertence.

eg.

- The driver's *negligence* led to the accident.
- The old grandmother felt *ignored* by the rest of her family.

Ant – Care, attention, heed.

eg.

- Tanisha takes good *care* of her plants.

- Mini's *attention* kept wandering in the chemistry class.

Nervous

Syn – Hesitant, timid, agitated, anxious, worried, edgy, jumpy, shaky, timorous, afraid.

eg.

- Shirish was quite *anxious* before his first train journey.
- Neva felt *worried* about her exam result.

Ant – Courageous, bold, manly, undaunted, valiant, brave.

eg.

- Shivaji was a *courageous* warrior.

- The *valiant* Rani of Jhansi fought the war very bravely.

New

Syn – Unused, fresh, novel, original, innovative, recent, latest, modern.

eg.

- This shop bakes *fresh* bread and cakes.
- *Modern* technology has alienated us more than it has connected.

Ant – Old, ancient, aged, obsolete, antique, antiquated.

eg.

- In today's day and age technology becomes *obsolete* so fast.
- In *ancient* India, education was imparted in the 'gurukuls'.

Nimble

Syn – Active, agile, lively, prompt, flexible, quick, speedy, spry, swift.

eg.

- The old gentleman stays *active* throughout the day.
- It is difficult to catch a cheetah since it is so *agile*.

Ant – Clumsy, sluggish, inert, inactive, dull.

eg.

- The *clumsy* servant dropped the crystal vase while cleaning it.
- The lazy boy lay *inert* on the couch watching television the whole afternoon.

Noble

Syn – Dignified, lofty, fine, gracious, eminent, honorable, great, illustrious, elevated, peer, lord, aristocrat, grand, magnificent.

eg.

- The *aristocrat* donated a large sum to a charity.
- Dibakar belongs to an *illustrious* family of singers.

Ant – Ignoble, mean, humble, trashy, common.

eg.

- The big star was proud of his *humble* origins.
- The price rise has hit the *common* man the most.

Note

Syn – Comment, obiter, dictum, observation, commentary, distinction, fame, glory, prestige, melody, tune, index, indication, mark, heed, notice, remark, detect, discern.

eg.

- The state conferred the highest *distinction* on the deserving student.
- The boy paid *heed* to his uncle's advice.

Noxious

Syn – Baneful, toxic, deadly, pestilent, virulent, malignant, pernicious.

eg.

- The *toxic* fumes from the factory posed a serious health hazard.

- The *deadly* virus was controlled by the timely action of the doctors.

Ant – Medicinal, remedial.

eg.

- Naturopathy encourages the treatment of diseases with herbs which have *medicinal* properties.
- The government has taken *remedial* measures to increase the usefulness of the Education Bill.

O

Oasis

Syn – Retreat, refuge, haven, sanctuary.

eg.

- The neighbourhood park was an *oasis* of serene tranquility.
- The Pandavas sought *refuge* in the jungle.

Oath

Syn – Pledge, vow, promise, curse, expletive.

eg.

- Bhishma took the *vow* of celibacy to fulfill his promise to his step-mother.

- Father *cursed* under his breath when he tripped on the cat

Obedient

Syn – Submissive, deferential, compliant, respectful, subservient, dutiful, tractable, yielding.

eg.

- The young queen was quite *submissive*.
- Students are expected to be *respectful* towards the teachers.

Ant – Mutinous, stubborn, intractable, disobedient.

eg.

- The *mutinous* rebels set fire to the buildings.
- The *stubborn* captain refused to leave his ship.

Object

Syn – Thing, entity, article, item, objective, aim, point.

eg.

- The *objective* of the game is to improve the team building spirit in the group.
- The police found a small metal *object* near the body.

Obligation

Syn – Duty, function, office, responsibility.

eg.

- A soldier's *duty* comes before his life.

- The President's *office* entails many responsibilities.

Oblivious

Syn – Forgetful, abstracted, absent-minded, inattentive.

eg.

- Our *absent minded* professor never remembers the names of his students.
- The teacher was annoyed with Satish for being *inattentive* in class.

Ant – Attentive, aware, observant.

eg.

- The best way to safeguard our neighborhood is to be *aware* of our surroundings.
- This artist is extremely *observant* of the finer details.

Obvious

Syn – Clear, evident, visible, distinct, palpable, discernible, perceptible.

eg.

- It was *evident* that the Mathurs' estranged sister had not been invited.
- Her interest in the subject was quite *discernible*.

Ant – Hidden, masked, veiled, covert, secret, obscure, concealed, latent.

eg.

- The lovers exchanged *covert* glances.
- The police officer issued a *veiled* warning to the thief.

Obnoxious

Syn – Loathsome, hateful, odious, offensive, detestable, abhorrent.

eg.

- The minister's *odious* secretary repulsed me.
- Rajat's use of *offensive* language was disliked by all his friends.

Ant – Pleasing, lovable.

eg.

- Dwija has a *pleasing* personality.
- Naman's brother is a *lovable* little brat.

Obscene

Syn – Lewd, immoral, unpleasant.

eg.

- He made an *obscene* gesture with his hands.
- The boys passed *lewd* remarks.

Obscure

Syn – Dark, incomprehensible, vague, doubtful, dim, dense, muddy, unintelligible, cloudy, dusky, hidden.

eg.

- The professor's reply to my query was quite *vague*.
- The servant made *unintelligible* sounds when he was asked about the theft.

Ant – Apparent, lucid, obvious, evident, plain, straightforward, transpar-ent, distinct.

eg.

- His heart was beating so *distinctly* he thought everyone could hear it.
- My doctor is a *straightforward* guy and doesn't believe in mincing words.

Obvious

Syn – Clear, noticeable, evident, apparent, understandable.

eg.

- The most *obvious* way to reduce pollution is to

reduce the number of cars on the road.

- It was *apparent* that the girl liked Sudhir a lot.

Ant - Obscure, vague, ambig-uous, doubtful.

eg.

- The details of the poet's life remained *obscure*.
- Her words seemed *amb-iguous*.

Occasion

Syn – Time, juncture, event, incident, occurrence, chance.

eg.

- I've seen Leena with them on several *occa-sions*.
- Sandeep is saving this bottle of champagne for a special *occasion*.

Odd

Syn – Queer, uneven, abno-rmal, unusual, strange, irre-gular.

eg.

- The doctor told him that he had an *irregular* pul-se.
- It was *unusual* for my night watchman not to report for work on time.

Ant – Usual, match, even, parallel.

eg.

- Rohit tried to get *even* by kicking his friend back.
- He greeted the guests with his *usual* cheerful smile.

Onerous

Syn – Burdensome, trouble-some, arduous, tedious, tir-ing, oppressive, difficult, wearing.

eg.

- The laborer finished one *arduous* task before moving to another.
- The *oppressive* weather slowed the travelers down.

Ant – Easy, comfortable.

eg.

- The couch had very *com-fortable* cushions.
- Apara is very *easy* to please.

Ooze

Syn – Drip, drizzle, trickle, drop, seep, leach, leak, let fall.

eg.

- When she saw her father in the hospital, tears *trickled* down her cheeks slowly.
- The *leak* in the roof had to be attended to immediately.

Ant – Rush, pour, gush, flow, rain.

eg.

- The water *poured* out of the geysers at a great speed.

- The children rushed out of the classes as soon as the bell rang.

Opinion

Syn – Thought, idea, judgment, theory, dogma, mind, notion, speculation, verdict, tenet.

eg.

- Amar hadn't the foggiest *idea* how he landed up in the hospital.
- The *verdict* of the judge was final.

Opportunity

Syn – Chance, opening, occasion, break, prospect, turn, expedient.

eg.

- The athlete did not want to miss the *chance* of participating in the national level championship.
- The starlet hoped the director would give her the *break* she had been looking for.

Ant – Omission, lapse, neglect.

eg.

- My insurance policy will *lapse* if I don't pay the premium on time.
- The patient's family accused the doctor of gross *neglect*.

Optimist

Syn – Hopeful, confident, brave, bright, cheerful, happy.

eg.

- Neerja always looks at the *bright* side of a situation.

- The UN was *hopeful* that the Peace Summit would be a positive step in restoring world peace.

Ant – Pessimist, dejected, drooping, disappointment, cheerless, hopeless.

eg.

- Shailja is a *pessimist* and believes in the worst of every situation.
- Minu felt *dejected* when her application was turned down.

Orderly

Syn – Neat, tidy, trim, arranged, methodical, organized, uniform, graceful.

eg.

- Pran's approach to his craft is quite *methodical.*
- Ambika *arranged* the flowers beautifully on the table.

Ant – Chaotic, disorderly, untidy, messy.

eg.

- The scene at the stadium just before the match started was totally *chaotic.*
- The students' dorm was very *messy.*

Ordinary

Syn – Average, common, usual, commonplace, regular, medium, inferior, undistinguished, run of the mill.

eg.

- The *average* man in India has a life span of 70 years.
- Shahrukh Khan's new movie has a *run of the mill* story.

Ant – Extraordinary, uncommon, one in a million, above average, abnormally high, first rate, superior, distinguished.

eg.

- Einstein was an *extraordinary* scientist.

- Haley's comet is a fairly *uncommon* phenomenon.

Organize

Syn – Classify, arrange, categorize, manage, order, sort, marshal.

eg.

- Bina's boss asked her to *categorize* and *arrange* the files neatly.
- The plant kingdom is *classified* into classes and sub-classes to ease understanding.

Ant – Disorganize, mud-dle, bungle, dishevel.

eg.

- My old aunt stepped out of her room in a *disheveled* state.
- The gang leader asked the new recruit not to *bungle* up the operation.

Outbreak

Syn – Commotion, eruption, epidemic, rash, occurrence, tumult, insurrection, outburst.

eg.

- Anna's *outburst* at her brother's party left all the guests embarrassed.
- The doctors quarantined the patients to contain the *epidemic*.

Ant – Order, quiet, peace.

eg.

- The judge asked for *order* to be restored in the courtroom.
- The house was *quiet* when he returned in the evening.

P

Pace

Syn – Speed, velocity, rate, tempo, rapidity.

eg.

- The *pace* of our lives has become very fast.
- The *speed* of the hare was more than the tortoise, but it was the latter's perseverance which made him win the race.

Pack

Syn – Set, bunch, group, herd, wrap.

eg.

- He forgot to *pack* his razor.
- He took the ripe *bunch* of grapes.

Pacify

Syn – Appease, soothe, calm, mollify, mitigate, allay, compose, quiet, tranquillize, assuage.

eg.

- The vet had to use a *tranquilizer* to *calm* the agitated dog.
- Chanda tried to *mollify* her friend's hurt feelings by apologizing for her behavior.

Ant – Irritate, inflame, annoy, incense, enrage, exasperate, vex.

eg.

- Little Jack's persistent questions *annoyed* his mother.
- The lack of remorse on Vipin's face further *enraged* his teacher.

Pain

Syn – Throes, pang, ache, hurt, twinge, grief, agony.

eg.

- Her limbs *ached* after the hard day's toil.
- His brother's rudeness *hurt* his feelings.

Ant – Health, pleasure, well-being, ecstasy, relief.

eg.

- Both meditation and exercise contribute to our mental and physical *well-being*.

- The application of cold compress provided immediate *relief* to his aching joints.

Pardon

Syn – Condone, forgive, acquit, excuse, amnesty, forgiveness, overlook.

eg.

- The criminal pleaded to the judge to *forgive* him.
- Father was in no mood to *overlook* my sister's impolite behavior.

Ant – Condemn, convict, punish, retaliation, retribution, vengeance, penalize.

eg.

- It is more important to forgive wrongdoers than to *punish* them.
- Our company has a policy to *penalize* absentees.

Part

Syn – Member, fraction, division, element, portion, share, segment, section, particle, fragment, piece, disjoin (used as 'part way with')

eg.

- Atom is the smallest *particle* which can't be divided any further.

- All the *members* of our club are expected to follow a dress code.

Ant – Connect, join, tie, attach, link, whole.

eg.

- The *whole* school has to participate in the passing out parade.

- Communication technology aims to *connect* people all over the world.

Partial

Syn – Unfair, incomplete, limited, fractional, biased, restricted, predisposed, one-sided, inequitable.

eg.

- Shubhu's work was *incomplete* till the last day of submission.
- My European boss' racial *bias* was quite evident.

Ant – Fair, entire, complete, whole, just, impartial.

eg.

- Akbar was renowned for being *just* and *impartial*.

- The *entire* auditorium was filled with people.

Passion

Syn – Love, anger, fury, obsession, infatuation emotion, fever, desire, excitement, zeal, fervor.

eg.

- Bhagat Singh's *obsession* with the idea of a free country sparked a revolution.

- There was *excitement* among the students on the day of the match.

Ant – Idea, conception, belief, thought.

eg.

- Gandhiji had a firm *belief* in the principle of non-violence.
- Marxist *thought* found its supporters in Europe.

Passive

Syn – Patient, inert, unreceptive, submissive, flaccid, reactive, resistant.

eg.

- Drug *resistant* bacteria become difficult to treat.
- She was *unreceptive* to the pleas of her grandmother.

Ant – Active, alert, proactive, vigilant, watchful.

eg.

- The dog was *alert* and on guard the whole night.
- The *vigilant* neighbors informed the police about the theft attempt.

Paternal

Syn – Fatherly, caring, patronizing, kind-hearted, warm, loving.

eg.

- The *kind hearted* couple adopted the stray pup.
- His elder brother was a *fatherly* figure in his life.

Patience

Syn – Forbearance, persistence, tolerance, endurance, fortitude, calmness.

eg.

- He handled adversity with *fortitude.*
- Religious *tolerance* is the first step towards a secular nation.

Ant – Wrath, rage, annoyance, ire, indignation, irritation.

eg.

- Shraddha flew into a fit of *rage.*
- Father's *indignation* at the servant's conduct was obvious.

Pause

Syn – Respite, interval, silence, gap, hiatus, halt, cessation, intermission, lull, suspension, break, recess, wait.

eg.

- Harish decided to take a short *break* from work.

- There seems to be no *respite* from the heat since the heat wave is expected to continue

Ant – Continue, continuation, continuity.

eg.

- The make-up artiste of the star needed the previous day's pictures to ensure *continuity* of the same scene.
- The prices of necessary commodities *continue* to rise.

Peculiar

Syn – Strange, weird, extraordinary, bizarre, remarkable, odd, queer, unusual, rare, abnormal, uncommon, irregular, singular.

eg.

- The Verma's son suffers from a *rare* blood disorder.
- It was *unusual* for Nira to be out so late in the evening.

Ant – Natural, customary, normal, commonplace, usual, ordinary.

eg.

- The *natural* surroundings of animals is called their habitat.
- It is *customary* for Indians to greet their guests with folded hands.

Perfect

Syn – Flawless, great, wonderful, faultless, ideal, consummate.

eg.

- Tanny has a *flawless* complexion.
- Sambhav is a *wonderful* friend.

Ant – Deficient, imperfect, flawed.

eg.

- The children's diet was *deficient* in vital nutrients.
- My bathroom mirror was *flawed* and had to be replaced.

Permanent

Syn – Stable, eternal, unending, enduring, lasting, durable.

eg.

- The orphan boy longed for a *stable* home and family life.
- Our teak doors are very *durable* and are expected to last long.

Ant – Brief, temporary, short-lived.

eg.

- Their *brief* affair ended when Naresh returned home after the holidays.
- Bunty took up a *temporary* job at the local library.

Permission

Syn – Leave, agreement, acquiescence, allowance, license, permit, liberty, authorization, consent.

eg.

- The husband signed the *consent* form before the wife's operation.
- The secretary was not at *liberty* to disclose the partner's name.

Ant – Prevention, refusal, resistance, prohibition, denial, hindrance, opposition, objection.

eg.

- Sonny's *refusal* to enter the dark room became the butt of many jokes.
- The defendant's illogical *objection* was overruled by the judge.

Persist

Syn – Continue, last, remain, stay, endure, insist, persevere.

eg.

- The cricket match *continued* despite the cloud cover.

- The poor woman *persevered* in her job despite troubles.

Ant – Discontinue, conclude, quit, finish, terminate, end, desist, cease.

eg.

- My mother has *discontinued* the use of aerosol sprays after reading about its ill effects.
- The session *terminated* without the parties reaching any consensus.

Persistent

Syn – Ceaseless, determined, relentless, continuous, unceasing, unremitting.

eg.

- Charu was *determined* to get the job.
- Yuvraj was *relentless* in his pursuit of his goal.

Ant – Occasional, sporadic, periodic, temporary.

eg.

- An *occasional* word of praise from the boss cheered up the young intern.
- The *sporadic* rain was insufficient for a good crop.

Physical

Syn – Bodily, carnal, corporeal, fleshy, substantial, material.

eg.

- Kings who became obsessed with *carnal* pleasures did so at the cost of their thrones.
- Despite being in a scuffle, neither of the two boys came to any *bodily* harm.

Ant – Mental, spiritual, intellectual.

eg.

- Neena is good in the *mental* mathematics class.
- Yoga and meditation add to a person's *spiritual* well being

Pitiable

Syn – Sad, distressing, sorrowful, moving, grievous, wretched, doleful, woeful, mournful.

eg.

- The news coverage of the war torn area was quite *distressing*.

- The news reader gave a *moving* account of the poor migrant's plight.

Ant – Pleasant, desirable, enviable.

eg.

- The weather was *pleasant* for this time of the year.
- Nikhil has an *enviable* collection of movies.

Plain

Syn – Clear, evident, simple, basic, obvious, natural, pure, conspicuous, apparent.

eg.

- My doctor advised me to drink aloe vera juice in its *natural* form.
- It was *evident* from the boy's face that he was lying.

Ant – Hidden, concealed, secret, imperceptible.

eg.

- The smuggled goods were *concealed* in the basement of the building.
- The child took the candy from me only when his mother gave an *imperceptible* nod.

Plead

Syn – Pray, beg, beseech, implore, supplicate, appeal, entreat.

eg.

- The pup's dumb eyes *implored* me to take him home.
- Ali *begged* his mother not to tell father about his report card.

Ant – Command, demand, order.

eg.

- The market's *demand* and supply determines the prices.
- The college authorities passed an interim *order* denying entry to the wrongdoers.

Pleasure

Syn – Delight, enjoyment, happiness, bliss, joy, contentment, ecstasy.

eg.

- The child's *delight* at being offered the second ice cream was a treat in itself.

- The enlightened person finds *joy* in small things.

Ant – Agony, pain, displeasure, sorrow, suffering.

eg.

- The princess felt the *agony* of separation from the beloved.
- Buddha believed that the cause of all *sorrow* and *suffering* is attachment.

Plentiful

Syn – Abundant, lavish, luxuriant, copious, plenteous, sufficient, replete, bountiful, teeming, lavish, ample.

eg.

- The accident site was *teeming* with media persons.
- Anuradha shed *copious* tears on being rejected.

Ant – Scarce, limited, niggardly, sparing, skimpy, scanty insufficient.

eg.

- The food supply was *scarce* in the war torn village of Iraq.
- Donna wore a *skimpy* outfit for the college party.

Polite

Syn – Elegant, genteel, gracious, courtly, refined, courteous, civil, polished, urbane.

eg.

- The *elegant* Maharani Gayatri Devi was a fashion icon.
- The thief's master was *gracious* enough to let him off with a warning.

Ant – Awkward, bluff, unpolished, uncouth, brusque, ill-bred, clownish, raw, insolent, insulting, discourteous, coarse.

eg.

- Puri was thrown out of the party because of his *uncouth* behavior.

- Doctor Wu was *brusque* and *discourteous* but an extremely good doctor.

Possess

Syn – Have, command, seize, own, enjoy, hold, obtain.

eg.

- The Bush administration did not *enjoy* a controversy free tenure.
- The star was arrested because he *had* drugs in his possession.

Ant – Want, forfeit, lose, need, dispossess, relinquish.

eg.

- The aging director agreed to *relinquish* his charge to his successor.
- The police *want* to catch the culprit as soon as possible.

Possible

Syn – Likely, potential, probable, conceivable, feasible, practicable.

eg.

- It was *possible* for any one of the four suspects to have killed the old woman.
- It was *likely* that the speech inflamed the protesters even further.

Ant – Impossible, impracticable, unachievable, inconceivable.

eg.

- It was *impossible* for the assassin to pass through the police cordon.
- Our teacher advised us not to set *unachievable* goals for completing our course.

Poor

Syn – Deprived, broke, meager, not good.

eg.

- She came from a *poor* family.
- The jacket was of *poor* quality.

Ant - Rich, wealthy, affluent.

eg.

- The *rich* man's joke is always the funniest.
- This is the neighborhood of the *affluent*.

Praise

Syn – Acclaim, extol, eulogize, flattery, approval, plaudits, cheers, compliment, applause.

eg.

- Imitation is the best form of *flattery.*
- The new haircut got her many *compliments.*

Ant – Abuse, vituperation, slander, scorn, obloquy, disparagement, reproof, contempt, blame, condemnation.

eg.

- The *contempt* on the girl's face hurt Vikram more than her words.
- The protester's *vituperative* language landed him behind the bars.

Precious

Syn – Costly, valuable, dear, invaluable, prized, inestimable, treasured.

eg.

- The *invaluable* Kohinoor diamond was seized by the East India Company and made a part of the British Crown Jewels.

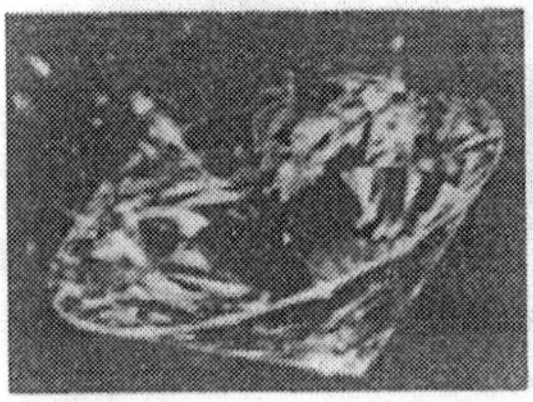

- Rahim wanted to present a *costly* sari to his mother.

Ant – Cheap, worthless, despicable, valueless, useless, paltry.

eg.

- Raima did not want to try out the *cheap* detergent powder.
- The police found that the forensic evidence was *worthless* in this case.

Predominant

Syn – Main, chief, prominent, superior, dominant, prevalent, prime, leading, major.

eg.

- Terrorism is the *dominant* theme of the movie.

- Sati was *prevalent* in India in the 17th century.

Ant – Minor, inferior, unimportant, junior, petty.

eg.

- The *junior* cricket team of our school won the match.
- The juvenile had a record of *petty* thefts.

Premature

Syn – Rash, hasty, unreasonable, early, untimely, precipitate.

eg.

- My brother advised me not to take any *rash* decision.
- The young soldier's parents mourned his *untimely* death.

Ant – Delayed, overdue, late, slow.

eg.

- The doctor wanted to observe him another day for any *delayed* response to the drug.
- According to the doctor's estimate, the baby was *overdue* by a week.

Pretent

Syn – Fabricate, sham, feign, imagine, imaginary, simulate.

eg.

- Surbhi *feigned* interest in the subject to impress the professor.
- Little Lola played with her *imaginary* friends.

Ant – Verify, substantiate, establish, authenticate.

eg.

- The servant was asked to *verify* his credentials.
- The government asked the official to *authenticate* the documents.

Privilege

Syn – Favor, grant, license, charter, immunity, exemption, right, prerogative.

eg.

- The police assured him *immunity* in return for turning witness for the state.

- True charity does not wonder if it is tax *exempted* or not.

Ant – Inhibition, veto, indictment, prohibition, debarment.

eg.

- The *indictment* of the terrorist came as no surprise.
- The corrupt lawyer's *debarment* made headlines.

Prohibit

Syn – Ban, prevent, preclude, inhibit, hinder, bar, forbid, disallow.

eg.

- Sati was *banned* in India by the efforts of Raja Ram Mohan Roy.

Ant – Authorize, consent to, direct, order, permit, enjoin, empower, command, allow.

eg.

- he Women Bill aims to *empower* the Indian woman.
- The night guard was *authorized* to carry a licensed revolver.

Prolong

Syn – Lengthen, continue, protract, extend, stretch, sustain.

eg.

- Radha plans to *continue* working after marriage.
- Shadows tend to *lengthen* in the evening.

Ant – Contain, lessen, shorten, diminish, abridge, decrease, contract, abbreviate, delay.

eg.

- My boss asked me to *abbreviate* the lengthy report.
- Her eyes *contracted* with suspicion.

Promote

Syn – Advance, help, push, urge on, raise, further, exhort, assist, excite, elevate, foment, advocate, encourage, foster.

eg.

- The professor asked Romi to *assist* him on the new course.
- Abhi tried to *encourage* his daughter to study further.

Ant – Allay, hinder, retard, prolong, discourage, divert, degrade.

eg.

- Bonsais are pruned in a way that *retards* their natural growth.

- With a great effort, Kamini *diverted* her gaze from the diamond necklace in the show window.

Protect

Syn – Save, cover, defend, guard, harbor, shelter, shield.

eg.

- When it started raining suddenly, all the people ran for *cover.*
- Today the pastor spoke about those who *harbor* animosity and ill will towards others.

Ant – Expose, betray, attack, plunder.

eg.

- The sting operation *exposed* the corrupt official.
- The traitor *betrayed* his country.

Prove

Syn – Justify, attest, bear, verify, establish, show, confirm, demonstrate.

eg.

- The police wanted the witness to *verify* facts.
- Ends, no matter how noble, can never *justify* the means.

Ant – Refuse, negate, deny, refute, repudiate, disprove.

eg.

- The star *denied* the allegations of her affair with her producer.
- Anubha pacified the guests in an attempt to *negate* the effect of her husband's tactless words.

Provide

Syn – Supply, prepare, afford, endow, grant,

furnish, get, arrange, cater, procure.

eg.

- Manu has loving parents who *cater* to all his needs.

Abhinav sent his mana-ger to *procure* the raw material for his factory.

Ant – Consume, spend, dissipate, exhaust, use.

eg.

- The hapless young girl *consumed* poison.
- Rajat decided that he would not think negative thoughts and *dissipate* his energy.

Publish

Syn – Proclaim, disclose, issue, print, distribute, advertise, circulate, announce, broadcast.

eg.

- The current *issue* of this magazine has a supplement on healthcare.
- The publisher decided to *print* an abridged version of the classic Moby Dick.

Punish

Syn – Afflict, chasten, penalize, rebuke, reprove, subdue, humble, chastise, correct, discipline, castigate.

eg.

- The principal *rebuked* the students responsible for the prank.
- Mother *castigated* my sister was getting such poor grades.

Ant – Recompense, reward, repay, compensate, remunerate.

eg.

- Mrinal agreed to *repay* the loan within ninety days.
- The police announced a handsome *reward* for any news of the dreaded dacoit.

Purpose

Syn – Aim, reason, rationale, point, idea, object, plan, intention, end, meaning, intent, resolve.

eg.

- Her *aim* was to hurt her enemy in every way possible.

- Swaran *resolved* to stay out of trouble.

Ant – Vague, aimless, unplanned, meaningless.

eg.

- Shuchi had a *vague* idea about the location of her friend's house.
- The *aimless* meandering of the girl's conversation left him confused.

Push

Syn – Press, thrust, shove, ram, urge, drive, propel, impel, jostle.

eg.

- The drunk driver *rammed* his car into the big truck.

- Shahana *jostled* for space in the crowded bus.

Ant – Pull, haul, drag, tow, tug.

eg.

- The contractor used levers and pulleys to *haul* heavy material on the top floors.
- Farzan *dragged* his heavy school bag behind him.

Q

Quack

Syn – Impostor, con, fraud, fake.

eg.

- One should beware of *quacks* selling quick fix remedies for everything from weight loss to cancer.
- The *impostor* was caught by the manager.

Qualification

Syn – Requirement, prerequi-site, condition, aptitude, skill, criterion.

eg.

- She had the academic *qualification* required for the university exam.
- Gehna has the *aptitude* to handle children.

Quality

Syn – Excellence, property, brand, value, worth, nature, trait, characteristic, attribute.

eg.

- It is unrealistic of parents to expect *excellence* from their children in every field.
- Our chemistry teacher asked us to learn the chemical *property* of all the metals.

Ant – Ordinary, flat, commonplace, colorless.

eg.

- '*Ordinary* day, let me be aware of the treasure you are.'
- It is *commonplace* in Indian villages for young girls to look after their siblings while their parents go to work.

Quantity

Syn – Measure, amount, bulk, number, volume, aggregate, sum, total.

eg.

- The sheer *volume* of the paperwork in the government office was staggering.
- Sonu sticks to the exact *measure* of the ingredients for any recipe given in the book,

Ant – Shortage, deficiency, insufficiency, deficit.

eg.

- Our company will have to cover the *deficit* incurred in this accounting year.
- *Insufficiency* of funds in the export house was alarming.

Quarrel

Syn – Wrangle, riot, fray, contest, enmity, fight, row, strife, controversy, brawl.

eg.

- The *enmity* between the two tribes led to a lot of bloodshed.
- The boys' mother had to intervene when they got into a *brawl.*

Ant – Agreement, assent, consent, harmony, friendship, peace, amity, equanimity.

eg.

- The new teacher's arrival restored *peace* in the classroom.
- The members signed a peace *agreement* at the summit.

Queer

Syn – Eccentric, abnormal, strange, odd, curious, peculiar, extraordinary, unusual, fantastic.

eg.

- It was *unusual* for Pete not to acknowledge my greeting.
- The suspect had a *strange* look on his face.

Ant – Ordinary, habitual, everyday, normal, common, usual.

eg.

- It was *usual* for his friend to wait for him by the roadside.
- Cows and dogs are a *common* sight on the roads in India.

Question

Syn – Doubt, issue, problem, query, investigation, interrogation, inquisition, inquiry.

eg.

- The suspect broke down during *interrogation.*
- The committee ordered an *inquiry* into the misappropriation of funds.

Ant – Reply, answer, rejoinder, respond, response.

eg.

- The teacher expected the correct *answer* from Simi.
- Pavlov's experiment on conditioning a *response* to a stimulus proved his theory of associative learning.

Quicken

Syn – Hasten, urge, speed, further, drive, advance, accelerate, expedite, dispatch, make haste.

eg.

- The driver *accelerated* the car and sped away.
- The old woman requested the lawyer to *expedite* her case.

Ant – Check, obstruct, retard, drag, hinder, impede, delay.

eg.

- Criticism *hinders* growth in a child.
- The teacher *checked* the boys who were climbing on the pillars.

Quiet

Syn – Repose, compose, lull, silent, mollify, soothe, allay, appease, stillness, calm, hush, quietude, rest.

eg.

- The atmosphere was quiet and *calm*.
- The mother rocked and tried to *soothe* the baby.

Ant – Excitement, tumult, rouse, commotion, turmoil, exasperate, disturb, aggravate, disquiet, enhance.

eg.

- The *excitement* in his voice was infectious.
- There was *commotion* in the hotel lobby.

R

Race

Syn – Tribe, battle, chase, pursuit, people, family, caste, nation, ethnic group.

eg.

- *Caste* system has been abolished by our govern-ment.
- My dog *chased* the neighbor's cat out of the backyard.

Rack

Syn – Stand, frame, bracket, support, holder, shelf.

eg.

- In the Nazi camps, prisoners were tortured on the *rack*.
- The carpenter could not fix the *bracket* to hold the magazine *rack* in place.
- I *racked* my brains trying to remember his name.

Racket

Syn – Row, noise, din, clamor, uproar, commotion.

eg.

- The old machine made an awful *racket*.
- There was *uproar* in the House of Lords when the motion was challen-ged.

Radiance

Syn – Sparkle, glow, warmth, joy.

eg.

- The artist was fascinated with the young face full of *radiance*.

- The couple *glowed* with happiness.

Ant - Dullness, dryness.

eg.

- Her complexion's *dullness* made her look older than she was.
- The saline water made her hair *dry*.

Radical

Syn – Essential, fundamental, thorough, drastic, sweeping, far reaching.

eg.

- The poll results were expected to have *far reaching* effects.
- Our constitution provides all citizens of India with *fundamental* rights.

Ant – Conservative.

eg.

- The elderly dean had a *conservative* approach towards education.

Raise

Syn – Lift, hoist, elevate, heave, haul, uplift, increase, promote.

eg.

- The school captain was asked to *hoist* the national flag before the parade.
- The janitor asked his boss to *increase* his pay.

Ant – Depress, descend, drop, lower.

eg.

- Aftab saw his junior *descend* the stairs.
- The real estate prices are not expected to *drop* in the near future.

Rare

Syn – Curious, extraordinary, odd, exceptional, peculiar, scarce, unique, infrequent, remarkable, unusual, uncommon, precious, incomparable.

eg.

- The poet was struck by the *incomparable* beauty of the young girl in the painting.

- Sapphire is a *precious* gem.

Ant – Common, usual, frequent, familiar, hackneyed, customary, trite.

eg.

- Hamid was *frequent* visitor to Abha's house.
- Salim found the *familiar* sights and sounds of his home very reassuring.

Rash

Syn – Hasty, reckless, venturesome, precipitate, indiscreet, incautious, foolhardy, hives, reaction, itchiness.

eg.

- The impatient young boy was a *reckless* driver.
- Cheryl's skin broke out in *hives* after she ate sea food.

Ant – Careful, wary, discreet, cautious.

eg.

- Red Riding Hood's mother asked her to be very *careful* in the woods.
- Jahnavi is quite *wary* of strangers.

Rate

Syn – Appraise, compute, charge, fee, price, estimate, assess, price, reckon, speed, tempo, pace, velocity.

eg.

- The *price* quoted by the vendor was way above Jayshree's budget.
- Our car picked up *speed* once we hit the highway.

Ant – Miscalculate, underrate, undervalue.

eg.

- Dinesh *miscalculated* the driving time to reach his destination.

- Chanakya believed that it was folly to *underrate* one's enemy.

Ration

Syn – Allotment, allowance, measure, quota, part, portion, share.

eg.

- Garv got admission in one of the finest colleges in the sports *quota.*
- The eldest brother got the lion's *share* in the family property.

Ant – Totality, aggregate, entirety, whole, sum total.

eg.

- The *whole* project was scrapped after the project manager left the job.
- Good looks are more than just a *sum total* of parts.

Reach

Syn – Arrive, attain, make, achieve, accomplish, contact.

eg.

- He has *reached* that point in his career where he can afford the luxuries he desires.
- The train *arrived* on time.

Ant - Depart, leave, take off.

eg.

- The flight departs at midnight.
- He *took off* for a holiday in the middle of the academic session.

Ready

Syn – Quick, speedy, alert, prepared, disposed, willing, set.

eg.

- The young girl was *willing* to marry a man of her parents' choice.
- The stage was *set* for the final act of the play.

Ant – Unwilling, slow, clumsy, unprepared.

eg.

- The little boy was *unwilling* to go home without taking a new toy.

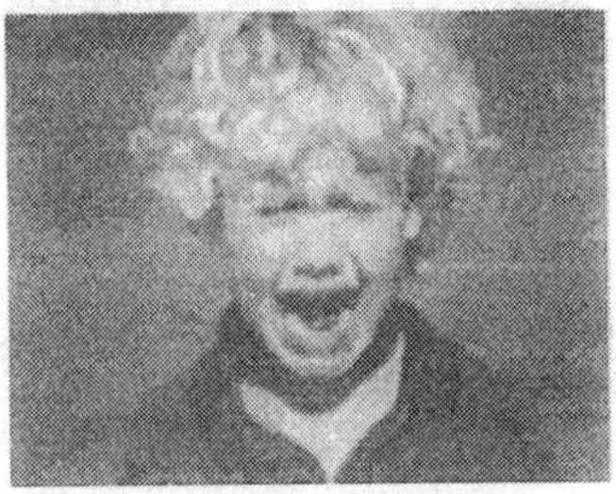

- The police car was patrolling the service lane *slowly*.

Real

Syn – Actual, genuine, true, factual, positive, authentic, certain, bona fide, valid, developed.

eg.

- The police asked him to verify that his credentials were *bona fide*.
- *Genuine* friends are true gems – rare and precious.

Ant – Conceived, reported, visionary, untrue, imaginary, unreal, fiction, fanciful, illusory.

eg.

- J K Rowling is the undisputed queen of *fiction*.

- Kushan's expectations for his son were *unreal* and impossible for him to achieve.

Reasoning

Syn – Rationale, thinking, logic, analysis, interpretation, reason.

eg.

- The scientist's *rationale* seemed flawed to the science community.
- Romeo's loved for Juliet defied all *logic* and *reasoning*.

Ant – Illogical, stupidity, nonsensical, senselessness, foolish.

eg.

- The *foolish* monkey trusted the crocodile.

- The *senselessness* of the whole exercise struck me afresh, and I decided to quit.

Rebellion

Syn – Sedition, mutiny, uprising, insurgence, revolt.

eg.

- The *mutiny* of 1857 was a precursor to the nationwide revolt which was to follow.
- The protesters were arrested on charges of *sedition.*

Ant – Loyalty, patriotism, devotion, faithfulness, nationalism.

eg.

- The freedom fighters' *patriotism* was exemplary.
- It is imperative to have *loyalty* to one's cause.

Recover

Syn – Heal, restore, retrieve, regain, resume, cure, convalesce, recuperate, repossess.

eg.

- Leela took another month off from work to *recuperate* after a prolonged illness.
- Honey had to fight a bitter custody battle to *regain* the visitation rights to his children.

Ant – Die, sink, worsen, grow, fail, replace.

eg.

- Mohini had to *replace* her washing machine after her old one gave way.
- The ill-fated ship *sank* in the infamous Bermuda Triangle without a trace.

Refuse

Syn – Veto, reject, snub, withhold, decline, turn down, rebuff, deny, repudiate.

eg.

- The celebrity *repudiated* the claims that she was leaving the country for good.
- She *snubbed* the suitor's advances.

Ant – Acquiesce, agree, grant, accede, cede, admit, assent, allow.

eg.

- My brother hated to *admit* his fault.
- He *agreed* to give another chance to his errant employee.

Release

Syn – Exempt, liberate, relieve, free, disengage, disent-angle, extricate, emancipate, discharge, let go.

eg.

- John tried his best to *extricate* himself from the messy legal proceedings.
- Paul was *discharged* from the hospital when he recovered.

Ant – Bind, confine, restrain.

eg.

- How closely we hold the very chains that *bind* us.
- The doctor asked her to take complete rest and stay *confined* to the bed.

Remarkable

Syn – Extraordinary, striking, significant, conspicuous, strange, distinguished, notable, famous, noticeable.

eg.

- Sunita was *conspicuous* by her absence at her brother's party.
- The urine sample showed *significant* level of pus cells.

Ant – Ordinary, commonplace, customary, normal, average, habitual.

eg.

- Vibha was the quintessential average looking girl next door.
- No man is *ordinary* to his mother.

Relief

Syn – Respite, reprieve, break, aid, help.

eg.

- He laughed in *relief* when he saw his daughter emerge out of the water.
- The cool room provided *respite* from the heat outside.

Reluctant

Syn – Unwilling, loath, slow, opposed, disinclined, averse, indisposed.

eg.

- The young mother dragged her *unwilling* boy from the toy shop.
- Gopal is quite *averse* to bunking classes.

Ant – Desirous, inclined, willing, eager, disposed, favorable.

eg.

- Tamanna was *eager* to join her new school.
- Nivedita was *inclined* towards vegetarianism.

Remains

Syn – Leftovers, remnants, relic, remainder, residue.

eg.

- The *leftovers* of the previous day's meal were on the table.
- The archaelogists discovered the *remains* of a mummy at the site.

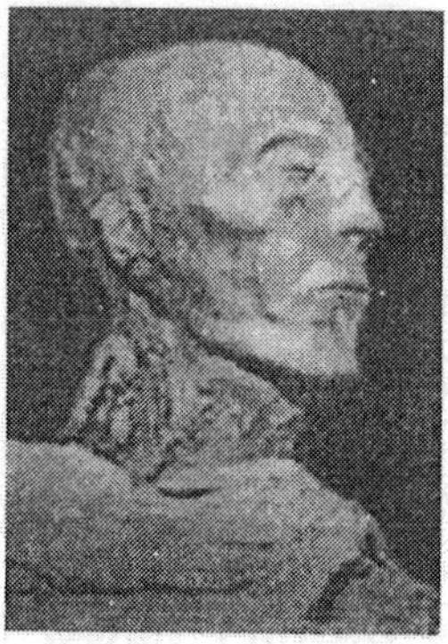

Repeal

Syn – Revoke, abolish, cancel, nullify, reverse, annul, rescind.

eg.

- The principal *revoked* the order rusticating Girish from school.
- Alcohol can *nullify* the effect of certain medicines.

Ant – Substantiate, endorse, confirm, ratify.

eg.

- Most celebrities *endorse* the vegan way of life.
- The doctor's secretary *confirmed* the appointment.

Repentance

Syn – Contrition, remorse, compunction, regret, sorrow, penitence, grief.

eg.

- Her *sorrow* was quite evident.
- Mukul felt *contrition* at his wrong action.

Ant – Satisfaction, complacence, pleasure, gratification.

eg.

- He takes immense pleasure in playing with his children.

- The new generation finds it difficult to postpone *gratification*.

Resign

Syn – Renounce, abandon, quit, leave, surrender, abdicate.

eg.

- Lord Ram surrendered to his stepmother, Kaikeyi's will and went to the jungle.

Ant – Hold, stay, continue, remain, maintain, retain, keep.

eg.

- The famous band, Strings, *continues* to rock the country.
- Krishan *remains* the number one heartthrob of the nation.

Respect

Syn – Esteem, deference, regard, reverence, admiration, consideration, accept (used as 'respect one's wishes')

eg.

- Ira has the highest *regard* for her father's wishes.
- His *admiration* for my sister was very obvious.

Ant – Contempt, disregard, ignore, insult.

eg.

- Shawn *disregarded* his doctor's advice at the cost of his own health.
- Ronit *insulted* his sister's boyfriend.

Retain

Syn – Employ, engage, preserve, maintain, keep, hold.

eg.

- Cleopatra knew the secret of *preserving* her good looks.

- The firm decided to *employ* a new lawyer.

Ant – Give up, cede, surrender, relinquish, renounce, forsake, abandon.

eg.

- The young unwed mother had to *abandon* her newborn.
- The inept chairman agreed to *relinquish* his hold on the company.

Riddle

Syn – Mystery, puzzle, problem, paradox, conundrum, brainteaser enigma, pierce (used as 'the bullets riddled his body')

eg.

- Agatha Christie has written some of the best *mystery* stories.

- More communication technology but less communication – this is the *paradox* of our times.

Risk

Syn – Hazard, jeopardy, venture, peril, danger, menace, threat, endanger, stake, imperil.

eg.

- Exposure to harmful fumes is an occupational *hazard* with factory workers.
- The policeman did not want to *imperil* the girl's life.

Ant – Security, secure, save, harbor, safety, defend, shelter, shield.

eg.

- National *security* is the first and foremost concern of our armed forces.
- We want to *shield* our children from all evil.

Rot

Syn – Decay, disintegrate, decompose, putrefy, become rancid.

eg.

- The police found the *decomposed* body of a young man in the garbage bin.
- The cottage cheese became *rancid* after a week in the refrigerator.

Ant – Flourish, bloom, grow.

eg.

- Trade and commerce *flourished* in the golden age of the Gupta rulers.
- Spring is the season of flowers *blooming* all around you.

Rough

Syn – Severe, stormy, coarse, rugged, harsh, bumpy, jagged, uneven.

eg.

- The *stormy* seas rocked the ship to and fro.

- Gus did not enjoy the *bumpy* ride on the potholed roads of the village.

Ant – Calm, glossy, smooth, even, fine, straight.

eg.

- The *glossy* magazine featured a hot shot model on its cover.
- There's a *fine* line between bravery and recklessness.

Rude

Syn – Discourteous, impud-ent, uncouth, vulgar, boorish, saucy, churlish, impertinent, impolite.

eg.

- The *boorish* young man was thrown out of the club.

- The girl was punished for being *impertinent* with her teacher.

Ant – Civil, cultivated, polished, courteous, elegant, refined, sophisticated, genteel.

eg.

- The *courteous* young woman told us the directions to our hotel.
- The *sophisticated* Ruhi Wadia was a role model for the young girls around her.

S

Sabbatical

Syn – Time off, vacation.

eg.

- Dr. Matthew is away on *sabbatical*.
- The actress decided to take some *time off* from her grueling schedule.

Sabotage

Syn – Damage, disrupt, harm, impair.

eg.

- The terrorists were planning acts of *sabotage* to intimidate the nation.
- The strike of the labour union *disrupted* the working of the factory.

Sack

Syn – Bag, pack, rucksack, backpack, dismiss, fire, discharge.

eg.

- He got the sack for *stealing*.
- She packed her *bags* and got ready to leave for a holiday.

Sacred

Syn – Holy, sanctified, consecrated, dedicated, inviolable, hallowed, divine, blessed.

eg.

- The *holy* shrine was opened for the public.

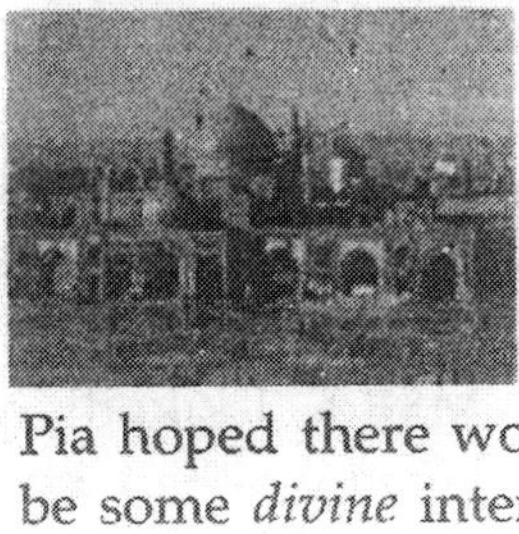

- Pia hoped there would be some *divine* intervention to save her from appearing for the exam.

Ant – Profane, impious, irreverent, irreligious, blasphemous, sacrilegious, worldly.

eg.

- Ravana was punished for his *impious* thoughts about Sita.
- Cutting one's hair is considered *sacrilegious* in the Sikh religion.

Sacrifice

Syn – Give up, forgo, forfeit, surrender.

eg.

- He *sacrificed* a promising career opportunity in the US to look after his parents.
- When Nagesh realized that he could not fight any more, he *surrendered.*

Sad

Syn – Dull, gloomy, poignant, grave, dejected, depressed, downcast, melancholy.

eg.

- Majid looked quite *gloomy* when he was rejected by the coach.
- The renowned poet was *melancholy* by nature.

Ant – Glad, gay, joyous, cheerful, excited, lively.

eg.

- Kamna was *excited* to see her aunt.
- The new boy in class had a very *cheerful* face.

Sanction

Syn – Allow, support, approve, ratify, endorse, authorize, permit, confirm.

eg.

- Our coach has *authorized* the captain to punish us if necessary.
- The driver had the *permit* to carry heavy machinery.

Ant – Disallow, debar, veto, ban, interdict, forbid, prohibit.

eg.

- Our teachers *forbid* smoking in class.
- Singapore has *banned* chewing gum.

Scatter

Syn – Sprinkle, fling, disperse, spread, broadcast, propagate, dissipate, disseminate, distribute.

eg.

- Joy loves to *sprinkle* water on unaware guests.
- The strong wind *disperses* the seeds of fruits and flowers to the far flung corners of the park.

Ant – Hoard, gather, store, amass, pick, collect, garner, accumulate.

eg.

- Niti love to *collect* memento from places she has visited.
- The wily businessman only knows how to *hoard* money and not donate it.

Scanty

Syn – Narrow, skimpy, insufficient, sparse, scarce, meager, limited, sparing, small.

eg.

- He is a man of *limited* means.
- The ration was *scarce* during drought.

Ant – Profuse, abundant, lavish, unlimited, sufficient, ample, copious.

eg.

- Her *ample* bosom heaved with emotion.
- The Kapoors threw a *lavish* party for their silver anniversary.

Scene

Syn – Sight, prospect, view, landscape, outlook, vista.

eg.

- This film contains some violent *scenes*.
- Lara took photographs of the beautiful *landscape*.

Scold

Syn – Reprimand, censure, reprove, admonish, rebuke, tell off, chide.

eg.

- His *censure* affected the students' performance.
- The teacher *admonished* the boy for not finishing his work on time.

Ant – Compliment, applaud, praise, commend.

eg.

- The audience stood up to *applaud* the speaker.

- Varun likes to *commend* his nephew to his superiors.

Seek

Syn – Hunt, court, inquire, request, look for, search, solicit, ask, follow.

eg.

- Lakshya courts *disaster* by driving so rashly.
- Purab likes to *solicit* women of loose character.

Ant – Shun, avoid, eschew, evade.

eg.

- Salim *shuns* publicity of any kind.
- The politician found it difficult to *evade* questions about his personal life.

Selfish

Syn – Greedy, egotist, self-centered, mercenary, ungenerous, egocentric, mean.

eg.

- The *mercenary* tradesman fleeced the customer.
- The big star was *egocentric* and arrogant.

Ant – Generous, liberal charitable, bountiful, lavish.

eg.

- The new government has promised a more *liberal* economic policy.
- This *charitable* institution looks after orphans.

Sensible

Syn – Judicious, wise, aware, conscious, intelligent, rational, observant, sagacious, cognizant, sane.

eg.

- The old grandfather was well known for his *judicious* choice of words.
- Mamata made a *conscious* decision to stay out of controversy.

Ant – Unaware, senseless, idiotic, stupid, asinine, foolish, doltish.

eg.

- The crazy man irritated everyone with his *senseless* repetition of words.
- It is *foolish* to invite a fox into your henhouse; one day he is bound to get hungry.

Separable

Syn – Divisible, classifiable, independent, branched, group into.

eg.

- Our class was *grouped into* smaller sets for the project allocation.
- Our genealogical family tree has *branched* off into three continents.

Ant – Unit, indivisible, united, inseparable.

eg.

- The twins were *inseparable* before marriage.
- A family is the smallest *unit* of society.

Shallow

Syn – Trifle, superficial, low, thin, slight, trivial, foolish, unintelligent, simple.

eg.

- The young bride suffered *superficial* burns when the cracker burst in her hand.
- The men discussed *trivial* matters till the women arrived.

Ant – Wise, intelligent, shrewd, astute, discerning, deep, clever.

eg.

- Mukesh Ambani is a *shrewd* businessman.

- The princes were taught by the *wise* sage.

Shame

Syn – Disgrace, humiliation, abashment, ignominy, infamy, dishonor, shyness, coyness, mortification.

eg.

- The Pandavas left the palace in *disgrace*.
- The young man could not bear the *humiliation* of failure.

Ant – Honor, grace, courage.

eg.

- A soldier fights the enemy to save the *honor* of his motherland.
- Akhil did not have the *courage* to tell the truth.

Shelter

Syn – Guard, protect, cover, refuge, sanctuary, haven, screen, defend, shield.

eg.

- The church provided *sanctuary* to the refugees.
- Jennifer took a parasol to *shield* her face from sun.

Ant – Betray, expel, reject, surrender, refuse, expose.

eg.

- Sujit had to *expel* the rowdy students from the school.
- The journalist *exposed* the true face of the self styled 'sadhu'.

Shock

Syn – Scare, upset, alarm, fright, distress, dismay, offend, outrage, blow, stun, surprise, tremor, horrify.

eg.

- The public *outrage* at the star's behavior demanded prompt action by the police.
- Sheila was *stunned* to hear about the young

neighbor's untimely death.

Ant – Delight, gladden, please.

eg.

- It was a *delight* to watch the young children play in the park.

- Sarah was *pleased* to see that her parents liked her young man.

Signify

Syn – Denote, suggest, connote, mean, imply, show, proclaim, indicate.

eg.

- Good marks do not automatically *mean* a good career.
- The boss wanted his gesture to *imply* that he wanted us to leave.

Ant – Veil, mask, cloak, cover, hide, conceal.

eg.

- His smile *masked* the sinister intent of his threat.
- Puran chewed on a gum to *mask* the smell of cigarette.

Silly

Syn – Absurd, stupid, ridiculous, asinine, inane, juvenile, senseless, foolish, unwise, nonsensical.

eg.

- The *foolish* girl believed every word the stranger said.
- It was *ridiculous* of Beth to expect her mother to baby sit every time she went out.

Ant – Sensible, clever, wise, sapient, intelligent.

eg.

- Birbal was the most *clever* minister in Akbar's court.

- Pam has a very *intelligent* dog.

Sincere

Syn – Genuine, true, frank, heartfelt, honest, truthful, earnest, open, wholehearted.

eg.

- The policeman was deceived by the *earnest* and boyish looks of the suspect.
- Jyoti had her parents' *wholehearted* approval for her project.

Ant – Affected, untrue, feigned, half-hearted, hypocritical, insincere, pretended.

eg.

- Minal *feigned* interest in the sci-fi movie.
- The socialite's *affected* and exaggerated mannerisms put me off.

Skill

Syn – Artistry, adroitness, expertise, talent, dexterity, proficiency, finesse, mastery.

eg.

- Anil's *proficiency* in the language got him the job of a translator.
- The art school polished Mauli's natural *talent*.

Ant – Clumsiness, incompetence, ineptitude.

eg.

- The new servant's *clumsiness* bugged Sangita.
- Monu's *ineptitude* in his job landed him in trouble.

Skilful

Syn – Competent, ingenious, adroit, clever, experienced.

eg.

- The writer was looking for a *competent* typist.
- The *clever* girl sidestepped the question very smartly.

Ant – Inexperienced, bungling, incompetent, clumsy, awkward.

eg.

- The *bungling* thief was caught red handed.
- The dance teacher was *inexperienced*.

Slander

Syn – Decry, defame, aspersion, opprobrious, accuse, malign, disparage, defamation.

eg.

- The wicked mother in law cast *aspersion* on her character.
- Veena tried to *malign* the good name of Tripti's family.

Ant – Praise, commendation, eulogies, laud.

eg.

- The commanding officer *praised* Aman's heroic efforts to save a fellow soldier.
- Jack showed me his letter of *commendation* from his previous employer.

Slavery

Syn – Subjugation, bondage, forced labor, submission, drudgery, servitude, captivity.

eg.

- The prisoner had been in *captivity* for too long.
- The king announced that he would release the slave from *bondage* very soon.

Ant – Freedom, emancipation, liberty, independence.

eg.

- The lawyer was not at *liberty* to discuss the affairs of his client.
- The US celebrates its *independence* day on the 4th of July.

Smart

Syn – Spruce, trim, elegant, chic, well groomed, well-dressed, tidy, immaculate, neat, showy.

eg.

- Mother was as *immaculate* as always.
- Ruth was the most *elegant* woman in the party.

Ant – Rugged, worn, scruffy, shabby, untidy, unkempt, threadbare.

eg.

- Vivian came to college unshaven, looking *unkempt* and *shabby*.

- The beggar wore *threadbare* clothes.

Slight

Syn – Ignore, disregard, neglect, small, unimportant, minor, trivial.

eg.

- Pran paid complete attention to detail, no matter how *trivial* it appeared.
- Mandira *neglects* her appearance.

Ant – Attend, consider, tend, heed, prize.

eg.

- Barbara wanted to *attend* to each and every guest personally.
- Pratibha *considered* leaving her job.

Slow

Syn – Gradual, dawdling, unhurried, leisurely, slack, retarded, sluggish.

eg.

- The boy's *unhurried* walk showed that he was in no hurry to get back home.
- The share index shows a *gradual* rise.

Ant – Agile, fast, quick, rapid, speedy, lively.

eg.

- The *agile* jaguar caught the unfortunate deer.

- His *rapid* ascent on the corporate ladder amazed his peers.

Sociable

Syn – Companionable, gregarious, outgoing, festive, affable, genial, convivial.

eg.

- Thenny's boys were quite *outgoing* and hated staying home.
- Raghav is an *affable* gentleman.

Ant – Secluded, inimical, hostile, sequestered, recluse.

eg.

- Robin was a *recluse* and hated meeting people.
- The court was not impressed by the *hostile* stance of the witness.

Society

Syn – Civilization, humanity, culture, people, public.

eg.

- The research studies the effects of modern technology on our *society*.
- The *public* cheered the cricketer when he came close to breaking his own record.

Soft

Syn – Plastic, squashy, flexible, pliable, yielding, malleable, supple.

eg.

- She admired the *supple* body of the young acrobat.
- The Montessori system is quite *flexible* in its approach to education.

Ant – Hard, firm, unyielding, compact, rigid, stiff.

eg.

- Mother was *firm* about my curfew time.
- Murli's father is *rigid* in his opinions.

Soil

Syn – Stain, spoil, dirty, smear, pollute, taint, contaminate, sully, earth, dirt, loam, mud, dust.

eg.

- The teacher warned Rahul not to *smear* his uniform with food.
- The director did not want to *taint* the reputation of his leading lady.

Ant – Clarify, clean, purge, wash, cleanse, purify.

eg.

- Forgiveness helps to *cleanse* the soul.
- Indians believe that a dip in the holy river Ganga will *purge* their sins.

Solemn

Syn – Traditional, sober, grave, glum, formal, serious, ceremonial, devotional, pious.

eg.

- Rita found the *formal* atmosphere at the college very stifling.
- It was difficult for little Ryan to look *sober* and serious.

Ant – Impious, cheerful, merry, jovial.

eg.

- Nikhil is a *cheerful* boy.
- The *jovial* mood of the boys made the party even livelier.

Solid

Syn – Sound, hard, firm, unyielding, concrete, reliable, trustworthy.

eg.

- The factory workers were *unyielding* in their demands.
- The police needed *concrete* evidence to convict the accused.

Ant – Unreliable, undependable, pliant, supple.

eg.

- Neeraj is an *undependable* friend.
- The ballerina's *supple* body twirled in rhythm with the music.

Solitary

Syn – Unfrequented, uninhabited, lonely, private, retiring, secluded, lonely, isolated, sequestered, deserted.

eg.

- Prakash's villa in Goa has a *private* beach.

- Indra lives on a *deserted* island.

Ant – Popular, well-frequented, sociable.

eg.

- Salsa is a *popular* dance form.
- The famous pub is a *well frequented* joint.

Solve

Syn – Decipher, decode, resolve, crack, explain, answer, unravel, uncover.

eg.

- I wanted to *unravel* the mystery of the missing silver candlestick.
- The famous symbologist managed to *crack* the code.

Ant – Baffle, confuse, puzzle.

eg.

- The students were *baffled* by the complex mathematical problem.
- The old gentleman keeps himself mentally alert by solving crosswords and *puzzles*.

Soothe

Syn – Palliate, alleviate, ease, appease, solace, assuage, calm, deaden, tranquillize.

eg.

- The weak king sought *solace* in the arms of the courtesan.

- The couple joined dance classes to *alleviate* the monotony of their lives.

Ant – Irritate, nettle, inflame, agitate, excite, stimulate, exasperate, enrage.

eg.

- My mother was *exasperated* by my sister's emotional outburst.
- Mohak was *nettled* by the incessant questions of his wife.

Soul

Syn – Mind, spirit, essence, core, heart, ego, vital, person.

eg.

- The warden wanted to get to the *core* of the matter.
- Ritwik's *mind* was a total blank when he gained consciousness.

Ant – Body, matter, embodiment.

eg.

- Sita was an *embodiment* of feminine virtue.
- The soldier's *body* was flown back home for cremation.

Spell

Syn – Charm, curse, bring, predict, imply.

eg.

- You've *spelled* my name wrong.
- The kiss of the prince broke the *spell*.

Spill

Syn – Fall, leak, dribble, trickle.

eg.

- I've *spilt* coffee all down my shirt.
- Crowds from the theatre were *spilling* onto the street.

Spin

Syn – Turn, roll, rotate, twirl, whirl, revolve, gyrate.

eg.

- The ball *spinned* out of sight.
- The skater *twirled* on her toes before taking a somersault.

Spirit

Syn – Strength, courage, character, guts, will, force, fortitude.

eg.

- Vivan was in high *spirits* after winning the race.
- It needs conviction and *courage* to turn down such a hefty bribe.

Spiteful

Syn – Mean, nasty, unpleasant, horrid, unkind, malicious.

eg.

- The *malicious* gossip hurt his reputation.
- The old neighbor was a *mean* and *nasty* person.

Ant – Benign, kind, compassionate, beneficent, benevolent.

eg.

- All religions beseech us to be *compassionate.*
- The *benevolent* patriarch forgave the young man.

Spread

Syn – Circulate, increase, swell, stretch, widen, broaden, multiply, distribute, propagate.

eg.

- Raji got the contract to *widen* the roads.
- There is no better way than travel if one wants to *broaden* one's outlook.

Ant – Accumulate, gather, collect.

eg.

- Little Mani went to the garden with her basket to *collect* flowers.
- He asked the guests to *gather* in the drawing room.

Splendid

Syn – Resplendent, fine, grand, wonderful, fabulous, superb, radiant, brilliant, beaming, shining.

eg.

- Her *radiant* smile lit up the dark room.
- The bride was *resplendent* in a lovely evening gown.

Ant – Dull, dark, dim, tarnished, cloudy.

eg.

- The stars looked *dim* in the *cloudy* sky.
- Her face looked *dull* and drained.

Square

Syn – Rectangle, cube, plaza.

eg.

- Her husband has a *square* jaw.
- The dining lounge was a *rectangle* shaped room.

Statement

Syn – Account, narration, proclamation, declaration, avowal, assertion, announcement, report, utterance.

eg.

- The director asked the writer for a story *narration*.
- There was an *announcement* in the newspaper regarding the postponement of the match.

Ant – Refutation, disavowal, contradiction, denial, negation.

eg.

- Rajeev followed a policy of stout *denial* every time he was questioned about his flings.
- His *contradiction* of facts was highly suspicious.

Steady

Syn – Constant, undeviating, stable, sturdy, secure, regular, firm, consistent, uniform.

eg.

- Tanvi craved for a job with *regular* working hours and *stable* income.
- Kumar was both *consistent* and hard working in his work.

Ant – Irregular, unstable, wavering, changeable, variable, unsteady, inconsistent.

eg.

- The doctor was concerned about his patient's *irregular* heartbeat.

- How can one feel secure standing on the *wavering* sands of fortune?

Steep

Syn – High, sharp, abrupt, sheer, vertical, precipitous.

eg.

- The *sheer* drop from the seventeenth floor balcony scared Anshu.
- The precipitous climb to the peak of Mt. Kilimanjaro has been attempted by very few.

Ant – Gradual, low, level, straight, easy, gentle.

eg.

- It is *easy* to forget a friend when all is going well.
- The *gentle* breeze swept the leaves away.

Still

Syn – Motionless, serene, peaceful, stagnant, quiet, calm, stationary, silent.

eg.

- The senior nun had a *serene* face.
- Children look so *peaceful* when they are sleeping.

Ant – Moving, excited, flowing, disturbed, troubled, agitated, running, flustered.

eg.

- Martina looked *flustered* when she was caught with her boyfriend.
- Anand was quite *disturbed* by the news of his brother's accident.

Stimulate

Syn – Instigate, whet, purr, rouse, kindle, inflame, goad, inspire, provoke, excite, fuel, encourage, incite.

eg.

- The leader tried to *provoke* the masses by giving an inflammatory speech.
- Tanmay tried to *goad* his sister into leaving the house.

Ant – Prevent, hinder, deter, calm, assuage, dissuade.

eg.

- Hari *dissuaded* his mother from stepping out of the house after dark.
- Yuri tried to *calm* his partner down after the big fight with the client.

Stimulus

Syn – Spur, incitement, motivation, inducement, incentive.

eg.

- The boy did not need any *incentive* to go out and play.
- The rider *spurred* the horse to run even faster.

Ant – Deterrent, dissuasion, response, hindrance.

eg.

- His *response* to the doctor's query was quite unsatisfactory.
- The high prices are a major *deterrent* in planning of holidays.

Strange

Syn – Extraordinary, queer, bizarre, unique, unusual, unnatural, uncommon, odd, eccentric, inexplicable.

eg.

- The disappearance of the ships at the infamous Bermuda Triangle is an *inexplicable* phenomenon.

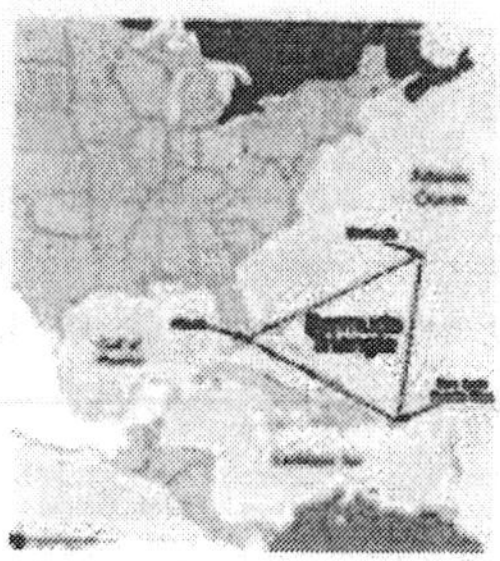

- The *odd* behavior of the waiter left us bewildered.

Ant – Normal, everyday, usual, natural, ordinary.

eg.

- Neha kept the items of *everyday* use in the shelf next to her bed.
- Rajni wanted to use *natural* products to make cosmetics.

Stop

Syn – Block, end, arrest, check, cease, halt, prevent, discontinue.

eg.

- The discussion *discontinued* when the participants started fighting.
- The infantry unit of the king took a night *halt* at the village.

Ant – Begin, activate, continue, quicken, purr.

eg.

- Archna had to *quicken* her pace to keep up with his father's strides.
- Kaavi went to the bank to *activate* her bank account.

Strong

Syn – Muscular, burly, brawny, strapping, powerful, sturdy, tough.

eg.

- The *strapping* young lad carried a heavy load on his back.
- The *powerful* king invaded his neighbor's kingdom.

Ant – Powerless, weak, soft.

eg.

- The doctor told Russy that he had a *weak* heart.
- The *soft* and colorful flower petals decorated the grass in my garden.

Stupid

Syn – Dense, dull, dim, thick, slow, brainless, dimwitted, thick, unintelligent.

eg.

- The young boy was so *dense* that his tutor just gave up on him.

- Pratibha behaves and talks like a *brainless* girl.

Ant – Bright, clever, intelligent, keen, smart.

eg.

- The *bright* little girl was the star of her class.
- My domestic staffer has become quite *smart* after moving to Mumbai.

Substantial

Syn – Actual, considerable, sizeable, extensive, ample, material, tangible, palpable, perceptible, corporeal, real, existing.

eg.

- The police had no *tangible* proof of her involvement in the scam.
- There was *perceptible* change on his face when he saw her.

Ant – Unsubstantial, illusory, unreal, shadowy, fanciful.

eg.

- Her husband's story about the missing bangle seemed far fetched and *unreal.*
- The *shadowy* figures in the dark frightened the little boy.

Success

Syn – Achievement, triumph, victory, accomplishment, hit.

eg.

- Their efforts finally met with *success.*
- The show was an instant *hit.*

Ant - Failure, collapse.

eg.

- There was power *failure* in the middle of the presentation.
- His plans *collapsed* like a pack of cards.

Such

Syn – Like.

eg.

- Characters *such* as Tom and Jerry are very popular with children.

- Giving birth is a natural process and should be treated as *such.*

Suitable

Syn – Appropriate, eligible, proper, right, fit, apt, pertinent, relevant, befitting, seemly, convenient, becoming.

eg.

- The suit was quite *appropriate* for the occasion.

- Vinod is the most *eligible* bachelor of our town.

Ant – Unsuitable, inappropriate, irrelevant, unseemly, untimely, improper.

eg.

- Daksha made an *unsuitable* comment about her friend's dress.
- The family mourned the *untimely* demise of the young girl.

Sudden

Syn – Momentary, abrupt, swift, brief, quick, unexpected, rapid, rash, unanticipated, unforeseen.

eg.

- Mahi had to use up the reserves he had kept aside for *unforeseen* contingencies.
- He stopped *abruptly* mid sentence.

Ant – Awaited, gradual, anticipated, progressive.

eg.

- The long *awaited* reply to my application finally arrived today.
- Virender was not disappointed since he had *anticipated* the outcome.

Suffer

Syn – Experience, bear, endure, put up with, go through.

eg.

- She's *suffering* a lot of pain.
- I could not *put up with* irritating relatives any more.

Ant - Enjoy, like, take pleasure from.

eg.

- She *enjoyed* her work a lot.
- Yuvraj *likes* to show off his biceps.

Summon

Syn – Call, invoke, bid, beckon, convene, send for.

eg.

- The priests *invoked* the blessings of the gods before starting the ceremony.
- The king decided to *send for* the queen's servants to find out the truth.

Ant – Dismiss, postpone.

eg.

- Naved has been *dismissed* from office.
- He could not *postpone* the decision any more.

Supericial

Syn – External, shallow, apparent, slight, surface, phony, outward, outer.

eg.

- The actor's *phony* smile was for the cameras only.
- It was *apparent* that the kid was very scared.

Ant – Thorough, penetrating, deep, profound.

eg.

- The lawyer was *thorough* in his questioning of the accused.
- Ramkrishna Paramhans wrote a book expounding his *profound* thoughts.

Sure

Syn – Certain, convinced, definite, doubtless, positive.

eg.

- Jugal was *certain* that the girl in the car had been his sister.
- The doctor was *positive* that the lab report was wrong.

Ant – Doubtful, uncertain, unsure, wavering, improbable.

eg.

- Our science teacher was *doubtful* about the outcome of the experiment.
- The girls were *uncertain* about where they wanted to go for dinner.

Surprising

Syn – Unexpected, shocking, astounding, marvelous, astonishing, amazing, startling, unanticipated, striking.

eg.

- The artist's canvas was a *marvelous* piece of art.
- The audience was enthralled by the *startling* finale of the play.

Ant – Everyday, ordinary, usual, normal, customary, monotonous, habitual.

eg.

- It is *customary* in Jehan's family for the boys to join their fathers in business.
- Hima found the work *monotonous* and boring.

Suppress

Syn – Subdue, overpower, repress, stifle, bridle, quash, restrain, quell, check, moderate, impede.

eg.

- The psychologist urged Bina's mother not to *stifle* her natural talent.
- The teacher found the little boy more *subdued* than ever.

Ant – Inflame, rouse, excite, provoke, agitate, kindle.

eg.

- My sister-in-law tried to *provoke* her mother.
- The advertisements tend to *excite* and titillate rather than educate.

Suspend

Syn – Debar, stay, hang, dangle, swing, postpone, hinder, stop, withhold, interrupt, discontinue, fall, defer, delay.

eg.

- The manager of the firm requested him to *defer* payment for some time.
- His lawyer asked him not to *withhold* any information.

Ant – Begin, keep up, urge on, protract, continue, expedite, prolong.

eg.

- Brij asked his lawyer to *expedite* the case.

- The family did not want to *prolong* the patient's agony.

Surrender

Syn – Leave, submit, yield, resign, yield, capitulate, waive, let so, give up, give over, cede, alienate, abandon.

eg.

- Javed *submitted* to his parent's will gracefully.
- The company *waived* off the employee's fine.

Ant – Withhold, hold, reserve, retain, detain.

eg.

- My friends *reserved* seats for me in the stadium.

- The police *detained* him for questioning.

Swell

Syn – Distend, puff up, enlarge, magnify, engorge, bulge, enhance, amplify, dilate.

eg.

- His abdomen *distended* because of the hernia.
- His chest *puffed up* with pride on hearing his son's praise.

Ant – Decrease, shorten, contract, reduce, diminish, abridge, attenuate.

eg.

- Stamina *decreases* with age.
- He did not want to *diminish* his chances of getting a good job.

Sympathy

Syn – Kindness, understanding, commiseration, love, pity, fellow-feeling, compassion.

eg.

- His *understanding* of the concepts of Physics was very limited.
- Her father advised her to show *compassion* towards the poor.

Ant – Pitilessness, cruelty, hard-heartedness, selfishness.

eg.

- Manish shows *cruelty* towards animals.
- The Muslim invader's *hard-heartedness* was well known.

Systematic

Syn – Methodical, regular, orderly, organized, efficient, logical.

eg.

- Anju *organized* her shelves regularly.
- Martha has a *methodical* approach to her work.

Ant – Irregular, causal, fortuitous, unmethodical, disorganized.

eg.

- His *disorganized* room annoyed his mother.
- Tripti was *irregular* in exercising.

T

Tab

Syn: Tag, flap, label, ticket, stub, strip.

eg.

- I'll put it on your *tab*, and you can pay tomorrow.
- The police have been keeping *tabs* on Raman ever since he got out of jail.

Table

Syn: Bench, board, stand, counter, desk, slab, chart.

eg.

- She has booked a *table* for five for 8 o'clock.
- I read the *table* of contents to make sure it had the required study material.
- The *desk* in my class was too low.

Tackle

Syn: Undertake, handle, attempt, deal with, equipment, gear.

eg.

- It took two fire engines to *tackle* the blaze.
- When I decided to *deal with* the problem myself, I felt a lot better.

Tail

Syn: End, conclusion, train, follow, back.

eg.
- The police have been *tailing* him for months.
- The dog wagged his *tail* in delight.

Ant: Head, top.

eg.
- He was the *head* of the security firm.
- It is one of the *top* engineering companies of our country.

Take

***Syn*:** Get, obtain, receive, acquire, catch, capture, win.

eg.
- Would you like to *take* a walk with me?
- He has *acquired* the taste for high living.

Talent

Syn – Ability, knack, faculty, genius, aptitude, skill.

eg.
- Rashmi has the *knack* for putting her foot in her mouth.
- Mahesh does not have the *aptitude* for an engineering job.

Ant – Inefficiency, inability.

eg.
- Rakhi's *inability* to voice her opinion made her feel frustrated.
- Shasini's *inefficiency* was responsible for their loss of the contract.

Tact

Syn – Finesse, diplomacy, discretion, skill, cleverness, consideration.

eg.
- The new salesgirl was smart but lacking in *finesse*.
- The minister was a picture of charm and *diplomacy* at the news conference.

Ant – Discourtesy, frankness, roughness, bluntness, simplicity.

eg.
- Rosy's *discourtesy* to the guests upset her husband.
- The police had to use *roughness* in dealing with the drug dealer.

Tasty

Syn – Appetizing, luscious, sumptuous, succulent, yummy, delicious, palatable.

eg.

- Naina laid out a *sumptuous* meal for her family.
- The chicken was so *succulent* it just melted in my mouth.

Ant – Nasty, sickening, nauseous, flavorless, insipid.

eg.

- Raj found the pasta *flavorless* and undercooked.
- The dish was so *insipid* that Rujhan could not eat more than a bite.

Tear

Syn – Rip, split, slash, lacerate, rupture, sever, shred.

eg.

- The victim had committed suicide by *slashing* her wrists.
- The dirt clogged and *ruptured* the drain pipe.

Ant – Repair, patch, rectify, restore, mend.

eg.

- The roof had to be *repaired* soon since it was going to rain.
- Father asked Ajay to *mend* his ways before it was too late.

Tease

Syn – Irritate, taunt, rag, rib, kid, chafe, provoke, vex, plague, torment, annoy.

eg.

- The little boy wanted to *torment* the cat.
- The termagant virago was always *nagging* her husband.

Ant – Hush, compose, conciliate, appease, calm, soothe, mollify.

eg.

- The priests sacrificed animals to *appease* the gods.
- Mother *soothe*d my anguished brow with her gentle touch.

Tempt

Syn – Seduce, lure, attract, coax, decoy, entice, inveigle, contrive, wheedle.

eg.

- The wily nautch girl *seduced* the king with her alluring charm.

- Carla tried to *wheedle* the state secrets from the inebriated minister.

Ant – Deter, disincline, discourage, restraint, dissuade.

eg.

- The high jungle gym did not *deter* the little boy from trying to climb it.
- The teacher tried to *dissuade* the weak student from taking science as the main subject.

Temporary

Syn – Fleeting, provisional, momentary, brief, passing, ephemeral, momentary, transitory, transient.

eg.

- The *brief* spell of rain refreshed the parched earth.

- The child's diversion was *momentary* and he started crying again for his mother.

Ant – Everlasting, immortal, invariable, permanent, persistent.

eg.

- Our body dies but the soul is *immortal.*
- She wrote her name on the book with a *permanent* marker.

Tendency

Syn – Prone, trend, bias, bent, leaning, proclivity, propensity.

eg.

- Neerja has a *proclivity* towards the fine arts.
- Manjhi is *prone* to respiratory ailments.

Ant – Aversion, distance, dislike, disinclination, antipathy, detestation.

eg.

- She has an *aversion* to liars.
- His *detestation* of the corrupt official was very obvious.

Terse

Syn – Neat, short, abrupt, brief, curt, succinct, laconic, compact, condensed.

eg.

- My boss gave a *curt* nod when I submitted my report.
- Her *succinct* reply annoyed her teacher.

Ant – Verbose, lengthy, wordy.

eg.

- Piyush is so *verbose* that it takes time to figure out what he is trying to say.
- Anuj submitted a *lengthy* report about the event.

Theory

Syn – Belief, premise, guess, postulate, assumption, speculation, doctrine, conjecture, hypothesis, supposition.

eg.

- The basic *premise* of the scientist's theory was wrong.
- Tarun does not like anyone questioning his religious *belief*.

Ant – Practical, realistic, actuality, happening.

eg.

- It was the *practical* aspect of moving out of his parents' house that deterred him.
- The minister asked the horticulturist to draft a more *realistic* approach to beautifying the massive colony park.

Thin

Syn – Diluted, meager, flimsy, scanty, sparse, skinny, slim, skeletal, emaciated, bony.

eg.

- The judge refused to grant them divorce on such *flimsy* grounds.

- The orphan looked *emaciated* and scared.

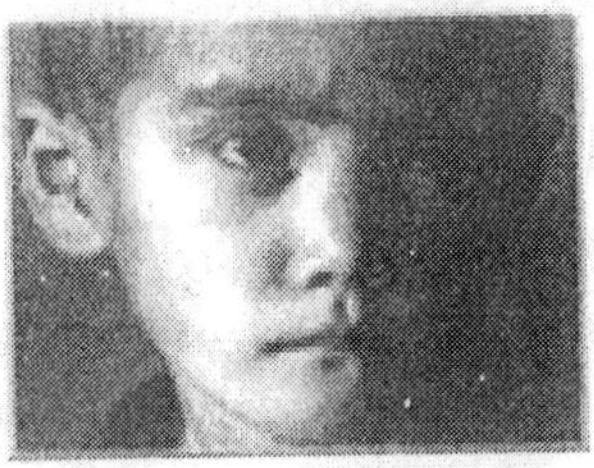

Ant – Strong, sturdy, bountiful, wholesome.

eg.

- The young man was *sturdy* as an ox.
- Our school meals are *wholesome* and nutritious.

Thoughtful

Syn – Attentive, circumspect, kind, caring, solicitous, heedful, prudent, careful, considerate, mindful.

eg.

- The new husband was quite *solicitous* and kept hovering around his wife.
- Sulabha was very *considerate* about her younger brother.

Ant – Carefree, gay, remiss, reckless, negligent, neglectful.

eg.

- It was *remiss* of the mother to forget her child's pram in the department store.
- She has become *negligent* towards her appearance.

Timely

Syn – Prompt, appropriate, apt, early, sensible, suitable, seasonable, opportune.

eg.

- She got a *prompt* reply from the publisher.
- Mickey waited for an *opportune* moment to tell his family about his marriage plans.

Ant – Tardy, untimely, late, inopportune.

eg.

- She was *late* in getting back home.
- Hiten's *untimely* advice to his friend was met with a stony stare.

Timid

Syn – Bashful, diffident, shy, nervous, meek, chicken-hearted, timorous, submissive.

eg.

- The *bashful* little boy hid behind his mother's skirt.

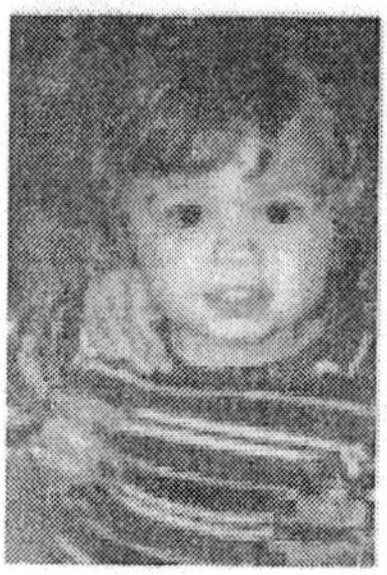

- The *meek* students did not check the teacher's mistake.

Ant – Audacious, daring, brave, confident, poised.

eg.

- The soldier's *daring* feat was an inspiration to the others.
- The young girl looked *confident* and *poised*.

Tired

Syn – Exhausted, drained, bushed, dead beat, fatigued, weary, worn-out.

eg.

- Susie was *worn out* by the end of the rehea-rsals.
- A day at the hospital with her ailing mother *exhausted* Sudeshna completely.

Ant – Strengthened, invigo-rated, refreshed, rested, relaxed.

eg.

- Regular exercise has *strengthened* the muscles of her legs.
- Shalini felt *invigorated* in the company of child-ren.

Tolerance

Syn – Acceptance, forbear-ance, temperance, endur-ance, laxity, forgiveness, clemency, moderation.

eg.

- Her mother expected her to show *temperance* towards the animals.
- The judge showed *clemency* to the hard-ened criminal.

Ant – Irritation, heating up, wearing off, rigidity, overbearing, dogmatism, fanaticism.

eg.

- Her husband's *irritation* with the guests was rather obvious.

- Anita's mother in law is quite overbearing by nature.

Topical

Syn – Contemporary, relevant, current, newsworthy.

eg.

- The *current* share market price index is a source of worry to most investors.
- I am a follower of contemporary Indian literature.

Torture

Syn – Anguish, pain, afflict, suffering, agony, torment, distress, persecute.

eg.

- The man was *distressed* to hear about his grandmother's death.
- The *anguished* eyes of the caged bear haunted me for a long time.

Ant – Allay, soothe, relief, comfort, palliate, ease, deaden, lessen.

eg.

- The pain *eased* after I took a pain killer.
- The scanty rainfall *lessened* the chances of a good crop.

Tragedy

Syn – Misfortune, disaster, affliction, calamity, catastrophe, adversity.

eg.

- The natural *calamity* was devastating and left millions homeless.
- It was the boy's *misfortune* that the hospital was so far from the accident site.

Ant – Farce, comedy, humor, drama.

eg.

- The movie we saw yesterday was an uproarious *comedy*.
- Rajbir likes to see *humor* in every situation.

Transparent

Syn – Clear, lucid, translucent see-through, obvious, apparent, crystalline.

eg.
- The *translucent* curtains seemed highly inadequate.
- The discourse was *lucid* enough for even the dumbest student to understand.

Ant – Foggy, obscure, opaque, vague.

eg.
- The morning was cold and *foggy*.

- The *opaque* glass was perfect for the shower cubicle.

Transient

Syn – Brief, fleeting, fugitive, short, flying, transitory, momentary, passing, ephemeral, temporary.

eg.
- Mark admitted having a *passing* fancy for the girl.
- She felt a *momentary* hesitation before confirming the date.

Ant – Long-lasting, permanent, persistent.

eg.
- He had a *persistent* cough for three weeks before he went to the doctor.
- He has a *long lasting* relationship with his girlfriend.

Treacherous

Syn – Disloyal, unfaithful, false, unreliable, deceitful, untrustworthy, perfidious.

eg.
- The lawyer granted him divorce on the grounds that he had been *unfaithful* to his wife.
- Davy was a *deceitful* man and Mona felt she could never trust him again.

Ant – Faithful, loyal, trusted, devoted, reliable, trustworthy.

eg.

- Her servant was *loyal* and dependable.
- Sharman was a *trusted* friend of Anushka's family.

Tremble

Syn – Vibrate, shiver, shake, quake, shudder, tremor, quiver.

eg.

- Vanita stood outside *shivering* in the cold.
- Leena *shuddered* to think of what could have happened if she had boarded the ill fated flight.

Ant – Stiffen, petrify, steady.

eg.

- Working long hours at the computers tends to *stiffen* the neck muscles.
- She tried to *steady* herself by holding on to the table.

Trick

Syn – Wile, skill, trap, scam, ruse, deception, ploy, imposture, cunning.

eg.

- The *cunning* fox ambushed the innocent rabbit.

- The man's sugar sweet words were a *ploy* to trap the unsuspecting girl.

Ant – Innocence, frankness, guilelessness, truth, sincerity.

eg.

- She had the *innocence* and freshness of youth.
- Robby could feel the *sincerity* in her words.

Trust

Syn – Reliance, faith, conviction, confidence, keeping, credit, office, duty, expectation, hope, credence, belief.

eg.

- He left the documents in his secretary's safe *keeping*.

- Ali had the *confidence* that Akram would never let him down.

Ant – Distrust, faithlessness, breaking of pledge, deception.

eg.

- The *distrust* on his face was the last thing she expected to see.
- Raoul's *deception* broke her heart.

Try

Syn – Strive, endeavor, aim, undertake, struggle, seek, attempt.

eg.

- The director urged the students to *strive* towards a better future.
- He *struggled* to keep his family together.

Ant – Leave, drop, quit.

eg.

- The defendant decided to *drop* the case.
- *Alice* quit her job after she was threatened by her co worker.

Tyranny

Syn – Totalitarianism, autocracy, oppression, despotism, rigor.

eg.

- Hitler's *despotism* led to unrest.
- The king's *oppression* made the people unhappy.

Ant – Pity, love, compassion, sympathy, softness.

eg.

- Leena tried to show *sympathy* to the small kid.
- The beggar did not like the *pity* he saw in my eyes.

U

Ugly

Syn – Homely, hideous, revolting, repulsive, plain, horrible, dreadful, unattractive, unsightly.

eg.

- The actress looked *revolting* without make-up.
- The old house looked *hideous* and haunted.

Ant – Attractive, beautiful, charming.

eg.

- Shashi's young girl was very *attractive.*
- Noor's daughter had a *charming* smile.

Unanimity

Syn – Harmony, unison, agreement, accord, concord.

eg.

- The crowd got up and clapped in *unison.*
- The members were in *agreement* of the motion.

Ant – Disagreement, contention, difference, variance, disharmony.

eg.

- The girl became a bone of *contention* between the two friends.
- Their views on the subject were at *variance* with each other.

Uncertain

Syn – Fluctuating, inconstant, unsure, vague, hesitant, doubtful, fitful, irregular, unreliable, changeable, precarious.

eg.

- Ridhhi saw a *vague* outline of a man standing behind the door.
- Their relationship stood on very *precarious* grounds.

Ant – Reliable, stable, trustworthy, unchangeable, regu-lar, steady, permanent.

eg.

- Shyam has been a *trustworthy* friend.
- Sandy is looking for a *steady* relationship.

Unconcerned

Syn – Nonchalant, blasé, apathetic, cool, carefree, disinterested, indifferent.

eg.

- Ranjan was quite *blasé* about his future plans.
- Manju replied to the headmistress' question with a *nonchalant* shrug.

Ant – Solicitous, interested, concerned, anxious.

eg.

- Kajal was *anxiously* awaiting the exam results.
- The doctor's *solicitous* query about her health made her feel better.

Unconquerable

Syn – Insuperable, invincible, impregnable, unbeatable, indomitable, insurmountable.

eg.

- The fortress was virtually *impregnable*, and the invader had to use elephants to break open the massive gates.

- The problem seemed *insurmountable* till he put his heart and mind into solving it.

Ant – Weak, powerless, feeble, conquerable.

eg.

- The *feeble* old woman could not even sit up to eat her food.
- The wise sages did tough penance to overcome the *conquerable* pleasures of the flesh.

Undertaking

Syn – Contract, endeavor, task, job, responsibility, trade, enterprise, engagement, venture, promise.

eg.

- Vineesh signed a *contract* of exclusivity with the film production company.
- Aarzoo had her husband's full support in her new *enterprise*.

Ant – Irresponsibility, refusal, truancy, escapade, avoidance.

eg.

- The boy's *irresponsibility* was a source of concern to his mother.
- Himaal's *refusal* to apologize to the girl's father landed him behind the bars.

Unfair

Syn – Unjust, iniquitous, inequitable, undue, excessive, unwarranted, partial, dishonest, wrongful.

eg.

- My math's teacher is *partial* towards the bright students.
- Vijay used *dishonest* and corrupt means to gain entrance into the college.

Ant – Fair, just, honest, unprejudiced, neutral, impartial, equitable.

eg.

- The sensible father did *equitable* distribution of his wealth among his heirs.
- The mediator tried to be as *neutral* as possible.

Unite

Syn – Combine, fuse, mix, bond, coalesce, blend, join, connect, amalgamate, knit, merge.

eg.

- The group was quite close and well *knit*.
- She tried to *blend* into the new group.

Ant – Scatter, disjoin, disconnect.

eg.

- The wind *scattered* the petals lying on the grass,
- The phone got *disconnected* due to poor connection.

Universal

Syn – All-embracing, common, total, collective, international, complete, whole, general, comprehensive, entire.

eg.

- There was a *collective* sigh in the movie hall when the heroine was rescued.
- The *general* public needs to be more informed about the electoral process.

Ant – Parochial, sectarian, sectional, factional.

eg.

- Narrow *parochial* interests go against the spirit of nationalism.
- The politician fanned the *factional* interests instead of encouraging patriotism for the country.

Unusual

Syn – Extraordinary, strange, odd, curious, remarkable, peculiar, uncommon, exceptional, singular, rare.

eg.

- The professor was a collector of *rare* scarabs.

- The Kohinoor is an *extraordinary* diamond.

Ant – Usual, common, commonplace, hackneyed, habitual.

eg.

- In India it is quite *commonplace* for married

sons to live with their parents.
- Harvey left for work at the *usual* time.

Uphold

Syn – Champion, back, support, sustain, maintain, endorse, advocate, espouse, defend.

eg.
- Malti decided to *espouse* the case of the street children.
- Raleigh *supported* his brother's decision to stand for elections.

Ant – Betray, drop, destroy.

eg.
- The prisoner of war did not want to divulge state secrets and *betray* his homeland.
- He *dropped* the idea of changing his job.

Upset

Syn – Disturb, disconcert, distress, disappoint, trouble, sadden, disrupt.

eg.
- Lady Asher was *distressed* by the sight of starving children.
- The young boy felt *saddened* at the prospect of leaving home.

Ant – Soothe, calm, relieve, relax.

eg.
- The child's mother was *relieved* at the sight of the approaching bus.
- The doctor asked the patient to *relax* and take a deep breath.

Urgent

Syn – Critical, pressing, vital, important, insistent, imperative.

eg.
- The doctor wanted to attend to the *critical* patient before the others.
- The boy said he had to discuss an issue of *vital* importance with the police officer.

Ant – Minor, inconsiderable, unimportant, trifling, petty, insignificant, trivial.

eg.
- The commissioner did not want to waste time discussing *trivial* matters.

- The accountant wanted to clear the pending *petty* expense.

Usual

Syn – Common, standard, natural, typical, accustomed, regular, customary, ordinary.

eg.

- The *natural* beauty of the village belle charmed the poet.

- He was *accustomed* to the moods of his boss.

Ant – Occasional, specific, unusual, unparalleled.

eg.

- The court decided on a *specific* date to settle the case.
- It was *unusual* to see her asking for help.

Utility

Syn – Service, use, advantage, function, profit, benefit, policy, avail, usefulness.

eg.

- Rahul had to climb the stairs since the elevators were out of *service.*
- Our family insurance *policy* is going to mature this year.

Ant – Disadvantageous, worthless, useless.

eg.

- The diamond ring he bought from the new jeweler turned out to be *worthless.*
- The new guard was fired because he was *useless.*

V

Vacant

Syn – Unoccupied, waste, free, vacuous, unfilled, empty, untenanted, blank, devoid.

eg.

- The gypsies parked themselves on the *unoccuied* piece of land.

- The big businessman signed and gave his son a *blank* cheque.

Ant – Occupied, jammed, replete, packed, filled, full, brimming, busy, crammed, gorged.

eg.

- The little kid *crammed* his mouth with food.
- Her eyes were *brimming* with tears.

Vague

Syn – Haze, dim, hazy, fuzzy, blurred, obscure, indistinct, indefinite.

eg.

- His travel plans were postponed *indefinitely.*
- She decided to go to some *obscure* village of Andhra Pradesh for a camping trip.

Ant – Clear, defined, plain, sensible, lucid, unambiguous.

eg.

- The lawyer was *lucid* in his explanation about the agreement.

- The event planner gave *clear* instructions to the servant about the party.

Valid

Syn – Defensible, suitable, applicable, compelling, powerful, efficacious, cogent, logical.

eg.

- The Indian Penal code has laws which are *applicable* to all citizens of India.
- Her argument was quite *compelling* and had to be taken into consideration.

Ant – Invalid, unconvincing, unsound, lame, feeble, weak, illogical.

eg.

- His application form was rejected because it was *invalid*.
- The teacher asked Anand not to give a *lame* excuse for not finishing his homework again.

Various

Syn – Different, multitudinous, numerous, countless, variegated, sundry, manifold, many, several.

eg.

- The chapel was lit up with *several* candles.

- The beautiful park had *countless* butterflies flying over the flowers.

Ant – Identical, few, exceptional.

eg.

- A *few* children bunked classes on the last day of school.
- The twins looked *identical*.

Vehement

Syn – Eager, fervent, heated, violent, intense, vigorous, earnest, passionate.

eg.

- The neighbors had a *heated* exchange of words.
- The *vigorous* exercise left him exhausted.

Ant – Feeble, mild, affected.

eg.

- She answered her teacher in an unsure and *feeble* voice.
- The boy had a *mild* case of chicken pox.

Victory

Syn – Triumph, win, supremacy, success, achievement, conquest, mastery.

eg.

- The Peace Summit was a resounding *success*.
- The king honored his commander in chief after his *triumph* at the battle.

Ant – Defeat, subservience, failure, frustration, descent, fall.

eg.

- Rani Padmini of Chittor committed 'Jauhar' after the king was *defeated* and killed by Alauddin Khilji, the Muslim invader.

- They preferred death to *subservience*.

Violation

Syn – Trespass, encroachment, infraction, breach, contravention, defiance, infringement, transgression.

eg.

- He was penalized for the *breach* of contract.
- The *trespassers* at the star's property were fined.

Ant – Compliance, adherence, concurrence, observance, acquiescence.

eg.

- The police expected the immigrants' complete *compliance* with the laws of the country.
- The master asked his disciples to lead a life in *adherence* to the rules of Buddhism.

Void

Syn – Abolish, negate (used as 'null and void'), nullify, cancel, revoke, repeal.

eg.

- The Indian courts have *abolished* the evil practice of 'sati'.

- The latest will *nullified* the validity of the earlier will.

Ant – Establish, endorse, legalize, permit, renew, uphold, validate.

eg.

- There is an ongoing debate about the necessity to *legalize* gay marriages.
- The owner refused to *renew* the lease of the premises.

Voluntary

Syn – Gratuitous, discretional, charitable, willing, unconstrained, optional.

eg.

- The *charitable* work she does for the poor girls gives her a lot of satisfaction.
- We were *willing* to take the risk of trying out an alternative system of education for our child.

Ant – Enforced, imperative, professional, compulsory.

eg.

- Laws are formed by the legislature and *enforced* by the judiciary in our country.
- Kiran agreed to provide *professional* advice to the law firm.

Vulgar

Syn – Coarse, lewd, crude, rude, earthy, improper, gross, obscene.

eg.

- Bhanu made *obscene* gestures to the drivers in the other cars.
- The boys passed *lewd* comments on the girls passing by.

Ant – Exquisite, polite, refined, polished.

eg.

- Her refusal was *polite* but firm.
- She is too *refined* to belong to the slums.

W

Wages

Syn – Payment, hire, pay, income, compensation, remuneration, salary, reward.

eg.

- He was happy with the *remuneration* he was getting.
- Fatima's *expenses* exceeded his income.

Ant – Expenses, fruitless, waste.

eg.

- Ratan did not want to increase his *expenses* any more.
- The students thought of the new experiment as a *fruitless* exercise.

Want

Syn – Indigence, penury, poverty, privation, desire, fancy, crave, covet.

eg.

- The rich man did not let his children forget his early days of abject *penury*.
- Samarth *craves* for fancy cars.

Ant – Affluence, plenty, prosperity, abundance, wealth.

eg.

- *Wealth* cannot buy good health.
- The *affluence* of her sister gave her an edge in her social circle too.

Wasteful

Syn – Prodigal, careless, extravagant, spendthrift, lavish, profligate, imprudent, reckless, unthrifty.

eg.

- The return of the *prodigal* son raised many eyebrows in the family.
- The *extravagant* party thrown by the Kapoors was typical of the nouveau riche.

Ant – Sparing, economical, prudent, frugal, miserly, provident.

eg.

- The old widow lived a *frugal* life.
- Our *miserly* grandfather was the butt of our jokes.

Wavering

Syn – Oscillating, unsteady, irresolute, dithering, fluctuating, undecided, undetermined, inconstant, vacillating, faltering, quivering.

eg.

- The girl's parents were *vacillating* between acceptance and rejection of the man's proposal.
- She was still *undecided* about which job she wanted to take.

Ant – Steady, unwavering, determined, firm, resolute, unhesitating, steadfast.

eg.

- Despite being in a long distance relationship, Anubha was *steadfast* in her affections for her beau.
- Raj was quite *resolute* about joining the army.

Weak

Syn – Decrepit, feeble, frail, puny, scrawny, infirm.

eg.

- The old woman was ailing and *infirm*.

- The *scrawny* little pup did not seem likely to survive.

Ant – Energetic, hardy, healthy, strong, robust, stout, sturdy, tough.

eg.

- The farmer wanted a *strong* bullock for his cart.
- The General looked *robust* and cheerful.

Weaken

Syn – Deteriorate, enfeeble, fail, decline, flag, wane, fade, sap, impair, debilitate.

eg.

- His eyesight *deteriorated* day by day.
- The picture *faded* from his mind with passing time.

Ant – Strengthen, fortify, brace, reinforce, harden.

eg.

- His term with the police force has *hardened* him.
- He *braced* himself to hear the worst from the doctor.

Wealth

Syn – Abundance, substance, affluence, material goods, riches, money, property, plenty, prosperity, possessions.

eg.

- The Bundela Kings enjoyed a reign of peace and *prosperity*.
- There was an *abundlance* of good crop that year.

Ant – Poverty, destitution, privations, distress, want, insufficiency.

eg.

- The government officials made a list of all the citizens below the *poverty* line.
- There was *destitution* writ large on the poor man's face.

Wet

Syn – Drenched, damp, humid, rainy, sopping, dripping, showery, moist, soak.

eg.

- The smell of *damp* earth was as refreshing as the showers.
- She got *drenched* in the rain.

Ant – Dry, arid, parched, dehydrate, parch.

eg.

- Rajasthan has hot and *dry* weather right through the year.
- Cactus grows extensively in the *arid* weather of deserts.

Wicked

Syn – Iniquitous, criminal, vile, villainous, corrupt, evil, immoral, bad, heinous, sinful.

eg.

- Ashok's *criminal* intentions were clear from the very first day.
- The court refused pardon for the *heinous* crime he had committed.

Ant – Virtuous, incorrupt, moral, upright, chaste.

eg.

- The *virtuous* queen refused to leave her husband's side.
- Sita had to go through a test by fire to prove that she was *chaste*.

Wide

Syn – Expansive, spacious, large, ample, broad, extensive.

eg.

- Sanjana loved the *spacious* bedrooms in her new house.
- When she was agitated, her *ample* bosom heaved with emotion.

Ant – Narrow, cramped, confined, circumscribed, close, limited, small.

eg.

- Rita could never find her books in the *cramped* cupboard.
- The patient was *confined* to the bed.

Wild

Syn – Ferocious, fierce, natural, untamed, undomesticated, uncultivated, feral, savage.

eg.

- The *savage* expression on the hungry lion's face scared the trainer.
- The *uncultivated* garden was full of weeds.

Ant – Gentle, timid, harmless, domesticated.

eg.

- A *gentle* breeze blew her hair.

- Sukanya was so *timid* that her brother always managed to bully her.

Wisdom

Syn – Knowledge, intelligence, insight, perception, discretion, sense, learning, erudition, discernment, sagacity, prudence.

eg.

- The tricky political situation required *prudence* and tact.
- Swami was well read, and his *erudition* was a source of pride to him.

Ant – Stupidity, ignorance, silliness.

eg.

- His *stupidity* landed all of us in trouble.
- The *silliness* of the whole situation struck her anew.

Worthless

Syn – Cheap, base, degraded, insignificant, useless, rubbish, trash, valueless, despicable, paltry, contemptible.

eg.

- The starlet got an *insignificant* role in the movie.

- Mother told us that it was our turn to take out the *trash*.

Ant – Excellent, good, transcendent, estimable, costly, valuable, admirable.

eg.

- The thief decamped with *valuable* jewelry.
- Father bought me a *costly* dress.

X

Xanthous

Syn – Light-skinned, golden-haired, yellow-haired, fair-haired, blonde, fair.

eg.

- The *light skinned* boy looked quite feminine.
- Little Miriam is a blue eyed *blonde* beauty.

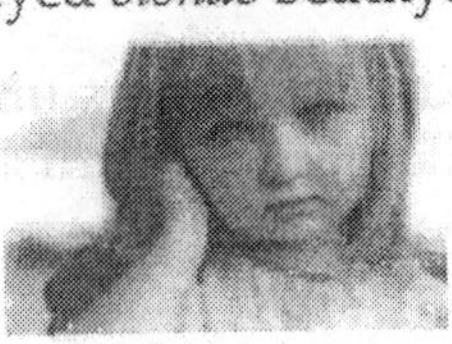

Ant – Brown, black, wheatish, thick- skinned.

eg.

- *Brown* rice is healthier than its fairer cousin.
- You need to be really *thick-skinned* to survive with my boss.

Y

Yawn

Syn – Gape, open, wide, part, split.

eg.

- The group *split* after a couple of performances.
- The couple decided to *part* amiably.
- I yawned uncontrollably when the lecture became boring.

Ant – Close, shut, abridge, shorten, peephole.

eg.

- The class was asked to read the *abridged* version of Thomas Hardy's classic 'Far From the Madding Crowd'.
- The censor board asked the producer to *shorten* the film by about thirty minutes.

Yeoman

Syn – Commandeer, volunteer, petty officer, selfless.

eg.

- Kiran *volunteers* time at the poor children's school.
- The chivalrous officer was awarded a posthumous award for his *selfless* service to the country.

Ant – Lord, governor, officer, landlord, boss.

eg.

- The *officer* was asked to step down after he was

involved in a controversy.

- The *landlord* asked Shinde to vacate the house.

Yield

Syn – Give way, submit, capitulate, acquiesce, accede, surrender, renounce, abandon, forgo, crop, produce, waive.

eg.

- The government decided to *waive* off taxes on farmers this year.
- The good monsoon ensured a good *crop*.

Ant – Resist, withstand, refuse, keep back, withhold, reserve, restrain, oppose, assail, contend, confront.

eg.

- The smell of burnt rice *assailed* his senses as soon as he entered the house.
- The key witness tried to *withhold* crucial information about the case.

Yoke

Syn – Link, couple, repression, burden, bondage, string.

eg.

- The *repression* of the farmers by the feudal lords led to a revolt.
- The ox has been a trusted beast of *burden* for ages.

Ant – Release, divorce, abandon.

eg.

- The couple realized that they couldn't live together and applied for a *divorce*.
- The young shepherd sang with a gay *abandon*.

Young

Syn – Youthful, boyish, new, fresh, juvenile, immature, infantile, childish, recent.

eg.

- The celebrity prided herself on her *youthful* looks.
- She found her groom *immature* and insensitive.

Ant – Mature, elderly, ripe, aged, late, full.

eg.

- Yachint is quite *mature* for his age.
- Her grandfather lived till the *ripe* old age of ninety.

Yowl

Syn – Bay, howl, moan, wail, bawl, blubber.

eg.

- The wind *howled* across the stormy sea.
- The little kitten *moaned* in pain.

Ant – Laughter.

eg.

- Their *laughter* rang out across the room.

Z

Zany

Syn – Crazy, madcap, whacky, buffoon, clown.

eg.

- The *crazy* fan was stalking the star.
- The girls were so *whacky* that the teacher kept laughing right through the trip.

Ant – Serious.

eg.

- Mother wanted her to become more *serious* about her studies.

Zap

Syn – Cut, finish, destroy, slay, liquidate, wipe - out.

eg.

- The brave prince set out to *slay* the evil demon.
- The aliens wanted to *wipe out* the entire planet.

Zeal

Syn – Zest, dedication, eagerness, earnestness, devotion, warmth, energy.

eg.

- Suraj brings a *dedication* to his work which is infectious.
- Father was happy to see Dhruv's *eagerness* to take on the new job.

Ant – Coolness, weakness, laziness, carelessness, apathy.

eg.

- It was sheer *laziness* on Shaurya's part that made him stay glued to the television.

- Citizens' *apathy* towards civic issues is quite disheartening.

Zenith

Syn – Peak, summit, peak, top, acme, height, climax, prime, heyday.

eg.

- The actress was well past her *prime.*
- The mountaineer wanted to reach the *peak* by the evening.

Ant – Nadir, base, depth, pit.

eg.

- The actor had hit the *nadir* in his career.
- The CEO had started at the *base* of the company ladder.

Zephyr

Syn – Air, blast, breeze, gust, gentle wind, flow, draft.

eg.

- The *draft* hit his face when he opened the door.
- The *gust* of wind blew the grain.

Zero

Syn – Naught, null, cipher, nothing, nil.

eg.

- The tutor's well meant efforts came to *naught*

with the indolent student.

- The man peered hard but could see *nothing* in the dark.

Ant – Infinite, zillion.

eg.

- Mother told little Shrey that the sky was home to *infinite* stars.

- Aparna always had a *zillion* worries on her mind.

Zest

Syn – Relish, gusto, appetite, liking, thrill, flavor, savor, twang, pep, dash, zing.

eg.

- She ate the food with *gusto*.
- I *relished* the salad.

Ant – Lethargy, indifference.

eg.

- He tried to fight *lethargy* by forcing himself to go for a game of basketball.
- Her *indifference* to her sister's plight was saddening.

Zip

Syn – Energy, force, steam, power, bounce, verve, rocket, vigor, dash, hasten, run, whirl, whiz.

eg.

- The *ball* bounced out of sight.
- The boy *dashed* out of the house.

Zonked

Syn – Besotted, looped, plastered, drunken, stoned, inebriated.

eg.

- Alauddin Khilji was *besotted* by the beautiful Rani Padmini.
- The *drunken* man fell down in the ditch.

Ant – Serious, sober.

eg.

- The elder of the two siblings is *sober*.
- Father was *serious* about sending me to the hostel if I did not do well in my exams.